Not Your
Usual Halacha

Volume IX

RABBI YAIR HOFFMAN

395 Oakland Avenue
Cedarhurst, NY 11516
516-374-9293
www.kbyt.org

Rabbi Yaakov Feitman
Morah D'Asrah

Avrumi Zelmanovitz
President
Daniel Burg
Vice President
Avi Pifko
Gabbai
Yoel Goldfeder
Secretary
Michoel Greenfield
Treasurer

ראש חדש טבת תשע"ה
נר שביעי

Chazal tell us אסתכל באורייתא וברא עלמא - Hashem looked into the Torah and created the world. This famous statement implies that everything in the universe can be found, in one form or another, in the Torah. Rabbi Yair Hoffman's amazing series of books *Not Your Usual Halacha* (so far in four volumes, a fifth in preparation) brilliantly illustrates this declaration. Written with both wit and brevity, they prove irrefutably, time after time, that the Torah and especially Halacha has something definitive to say about every event, phenomenon, issue, societal trend and ethical dilemma in the world.

With his vast encyclopedic knowledge and ability to apply the ancient to the modern, Rabbi Hoffman authoritatively addresses such disparate subjects as Yeshiva tuition, dangerous cults, bugs in our food, Ebola, ebay, Six-legged calves, tyrant bosses, Ponzi schemes, the Pope's yarmulka and dozens more. Both scholar and layman will gain tremendously from this erudite and entertaining series, and most important, will surely be inspired to study and learn more Torah and apply it to our everyday lives.

With all best wishes,

כ' ידיד (אך נ' אוי' אי' (נ') שם)

Sincerely,

Rabbi Yaakov Feitman

מהסכמות של ספריו של המחבר על ספר לפני עוור ונדפס כאן ברשות הראש ישיבה

בס"ד

RABBI ARYEH MALKIEL KOTLER
BETH MEDRASH GOVOHA
LAKEWOOD, N.J. 08701

אריה מלכיאל קוטלר
בית מדרש גבוה
לייקוואוד, נ. דז.

ג' אב תשע"ט

במדרש ויק"ר פכ"ד ה' פרשת קדושים נאמרה בהקהל מפני שרוב
הלכות [illegible] בתורה [illegible] ע"ש ומובא ברמב"ן [illegible] ובביאור הדבר
[illegible] עשרת הדברות [illegible] בדברי הברית והיינו [illegible] את הכלל
[illegible] ומרוממין ומעלין אותן, והנה בתוך [illegible] שקדושים [illegible]
[illegible] קדושה כדוגמת קידושי איש ואשה, ודוגמא כזה [illegible] בגלוי
[illegible] שנתקדשו [illegible] בלי תמורה אל דם רעיך ובלא תחמוד [illegible] ואהבת
לרעך כמוך ועל כן נאמרה בהקהל אנשים נשים וטף, ואף גם לפני עור
בכלל, [illegible] שמבואר [illegible] לפרוק בו ביום [illegible], ע"ש.

ע"כ [illegible] ידידי הרה"ג ר' [illegible] שליט"א
אשר חיבר ספר [illegible] לפני עור בשם [illegible]
[illegible], בספר המבוסס המקיף את כל דיני [illegible]
והנהגה להלכה [illegible] עם [illegible] של כל, [illegible]
[illegible] המספיק על פסקי הלכות [illegible]
ונאמנים [illegible] דברי הגאון ר' דוב [illegible] שליט"א [illegible]
הסכמה, הרי יש בזה [illegible] תועלת [illegible], [illegible]
[illegible] ולרוממות [illegible] יתר [illegible]
בני מדרשנו [illegible] להגדיל תורה ולהאדירה

הכו"ח לכבוד התורה ולומדיה אריה מלכיאל קוטלר
[illegible]

This Sefer is dedicated in loving memory of

The author's parents

Dr. Nathan and Sarah Hoffman z"l

TABLE OF CONTENTS

Musical Cultural Diffusion And Halacha

Question: What do Yeshiva Bochurim and seminary girls, Spanish Salsa music fans of Marc Anthony, and French Muslim fans of Algerian Rai music all have in common?

Answer: They all dance to the very same music.

The Yeshiva boys and Sem girls all know it as the music to the song, "Hashem Melech, Hashem Malach, Hashem Yimloch l'olam vo'ed" which has taken the Jewish world by a storm and is sung by the dynamic Gad Elbaz.

THE PREVIOUS VERSIONS

The Spanish Salsa music fans of Marc Anthony know it as the tune that he used for his song – "Vivir mi Vida" – a song which happened to have earned a Latin Grammy in 2013.

And the Algerian Muslims all know it as the music for the Arabic and French multi-lingual song called C'est la vie by Khaled Haj Ibrahim of Oran Algeria.

The Spanish version was composed in 2013, the original Muslim version was composed in 2012, and the Gad Elbaz version was released in 2016.

WHAT DOES HALACHA SAY?

The question is, what does Halacha have to say about the fact that the music to one of the most popular Chasuna songs in contemporary times originally came from an Arab love song with decidedly un-Yeshivesh lyrics?

The Sefer Chassidim #238 states that one should not use a Nigun that was used for Avodah Zarah worship to use in praising Hashem. Indeed, it even states that one should avoid humming a good piece of music in front of one who is apt to use it in the worship of Avodah Zarah! While that is true with Avodah Zarah, does the same apply to songs that allude to impropriety or that have such lyrics straight out?

TZITZ ELIEZER'S VIEW

Rav Eliezer Yehudah Waldenberg zt"l, author of the Tzitz Eliezer addresses this very issue. He writes (volume XIII Siman 12) quite clearly that it is "an abomination to dress up words of holiness in 'malbushei tzo'im – soiled clothing' that give off an odor of promiscuity."

PERHAPS A MORE LENIENT VIEW

Interestingly enough, however, Rav Moshe Feinstein zt"l penned a response to a Rebbe who was teaching in Rav Binyamin Kamenetsky's Yeshiva of South Shore (IM EH Vol. I #96), addressing a related issue. The Rebbe, Rav Shmuel Dishon Shlita, had asked Rav Moshe about a certain individual artist who once had an excellent reputation. The artist had composed a number of musical compositions that had captured the hearts of the Torah community. Unfortunately, the artist had gone astray. Is it permitted to listen and sing the tunes that he had composed while he was still "fully kosher?"

[The issue has to do with giving a "good name" to evildoers which would violate a principle found in the Talmud (Yuma 38b.)]

BNEI TORAH AND BAALEI NEFESH SHOULD AVOID IT

Rav Moshe zt"l rules that there is nothing wrong with doing so for tunes that he had composed while he was "fully kosher." For tunes that he had composed after his fall, Rav Feinstein writes, "it is likely that we should not be stringent since tunes do not essentially have to do with matters of Kedusha, however, Bnei Torah and Baalei Nefesh should avoid it."

Rav Feinstein based his ruling on the fact that some authorities (See Meleches Shlomo on Maaser Sheini) are of the view that the Yochanan Kohain Gadol who had promulgated many decrees in regard to Maaser Sheini – was, in fact, the same Yochanan Kohain Gadol who eventually became a Sadduccee. These decrees, however, were made while he was still "fully kosher."

Rav Feinstein zt"l further writes that tunes, are essentially a matter that has nothing to do with a Davar Shebekedusha and should be no different than inventions of machinery or medicine.

MORE POSKIM WHO ENTIRELY FORBID

Rav Menashe Klein (Mishneh Halachos Vol. VI #108), without mentioning the view of Rav Feinstein comes to the exact opposite conclusion and writes that it is entirely forbidden to do so – even in regard to the tunes composed while he was still "kosher."

Rav Moshe Stern (Be'er Moshe Vol. VI #74 in the notes), the Debriciner Rav, also forbids the matter and even writes that it is forbidden to sell tapes of such individuals. Indeed, Rav Stern writes that one must even look into a person who would even stoop to sell such tapes. Interestingly enough, Rav Stern also does not mention the more permissive view of Rav Feinstein on the topic.

The Halachic publication of the Skver Rebbe's Kollelim (Zera Yaakov Gilyon #26) cites the more stringent view of Rav Moshe Stern in their halachic conclusions – ignoring entirely the view of Rav Feinstein.

It could also be argued that even Rav Feinstein might have agreed to the aforementioned view of the Tzitz Eliezer in regard to clothing words of praise in a tune of "soiled clothing," and that he was only lenient in regard to the underlying issue of giving a good name to evildoers.

MORE LENIENT VIEWS

On the other hand, the Bach in Orech Chaim Siman 53 writes that it is only problematic if the tune is generally exclusive to the Avodah Zarah. Otherwise, the Bach seems to allow it.

If, however, the origin is unknown to the Chazan or singer – then it could perhaps not be such an issue. A manuscript version of the Levush that this author once saw seemed to indicate this position.

THE ISSUE OF ATTRIBUTION

Another issue is attribution. Hopefully, whenever this happens, Jewish artists do attribute the original artist's contribution and not attempt to take credit for it ourselves. The Rambam writes in the introduction to the yad Hachazakah that some of the ideas came from a very wise man, but since people generally look askance at wisdom from a foreign source – he left the wise man's name anonymous. Most students of philosophy, however, can detect that he as referencing Aristotle. [The photo above was taken by Yehonatan Chevroni].

That same problem certainly exists in music too, and, as a result, parodies or modified versions of musical pieces usually hint to or allude to the original artist. The problem is when we do not attribute or at least allude to the original author we may be in violation of something that is quite clearly against a Torah value.

A famous Jewish song entitled "Yidden" was originally based upon the music of a West German band called "Dschinghis Khan" who placed their song as their entry in the Eurovision Song Contest of 1979. The composer of the original music was a person named Ralph Siegel. The Jewish song did, in this author's recollection, at least attribute the artist somewhat anonymously.

A famous children's singer took the music from a Clint Eastwood 1950's western called "Rawhide" – and did not, it appears, attribute the music to its original composer – even anonymously.

KING SOLOMON'S ADMONITION

King Solomon tells us (Mishlei 22:22) the following words: "Rob not from a poor person – for he is poor." Chazal tell us (Yalkut Shimoni Mishlei 560; Midrash Tanchuma BaMidbar 27) that Shlomo HaMelech is actually referring to plagiarism – to reciting a statement without attributing it to its source.

Just as a poor person has no protector – no guardian to right wrongs and injustices, the same is true with intellectual property. An earlier thinker came up with an idea. Just as the poor person has no protector, so too does the thinker have no protector. Shlomo HaMelech is appealing to our conscience – do not steal from a poor person – for he is poor – he has no protector. Do not cheat or plagiarize for they too – have no protector.

Queen Esther (Megilas Esther 2:22) informs her husband the king of Persia of Bigson and Seresh had plotted a coup d'etat. She informs Achashveirosh that Mordechai, proficient in seventy languages,

14

overheard and told the Queen. Queen Esther didn't take credit for the information.

She specifically told the King that she had actually obtained the information from Mordechai.

Esther was amply rewarded. It is, in fact, for this action that she merited to be the conduit of the salvation of Israel. Because of Esther it is said, "Whoever says something in the name of its originator brings salvation to the world."

What was really going on here? Esther certainly was a righteous woman. Can't we assume that if she thought it better for the king to have assumed that the information came from her, then surely she would have been fully justified?

WE MUST FOLLOW HASHEM'S BIDDING

It would seem not. It would seem that even though, it may have been in the Jewish interest that Esther gain the king's favor, there is something inherently wrong in not attributing the information to the true source. She knew this. Esther could not stoop to do something that is inherently wrong. It was for this realization — that we are but mere foot soldiers in a campaign and our primary responsibility is to follow Hashem's bidding in what is right and wrong that she was so amply rewarded.

A MEANS OF ACQUIRING TORAH

In Pirkei Avos (6:5) we see that naming the original source of the information is, in fact, in a list of one of the 48 ways in which Torah is acquired.

COMPARED TO KIDNAPPING

The Yalkut Yoseph (Kivud Av VoAim chapter 9) cites a few more sources. The Shla in Meseches Shvuos says that it is an enormous sin — and should be looked at as if one kidnapped human life. Kidnapping is a serious crime, but it seems that it is the parallel emotion that authors feel when their work has been taken from them without attribution.

PHOTOGRAPHERS AS WELL

There are other artists who constantly feel that pain as well. There are very talented photographers that work very hard to get a particular shot. Often media sources do not attribute the photographer properly and take the work without permission.

During the season of Pesach, where we are adjured to rid ourselves of Chometz, we should also pay attention to spiritual Chometz too – whether it is in the form of not attributing things properly or to matters that take us away from Hashem. Both of these items are a form of spiritual Chometz.

CONCLUSION

Rav Feinstein writes that Bnei Torah and Baalei Nefesh should refrain from using such music, although he writes that it is essentially permitted. The Tzitz Eliezer writes that it is forbidden, as do the Debreciner Rav and the Mishna Halachos. The Bach indicates that if it is used in other venues too that there is no prohibition. Each person should consult his own Rav or Posaik. None of this, of course, affects the essential truth of the declaration: Hashem Melech, Hashem Malach, Hashem Yimloch l'olam vo'ed.

The Shidduch Crisis and the Takannah of the Rabbis

It was a shidduch crisis. The young women were not getting married and a solution needed to happen. The greatest Rabbis of the generation got together and worked out a solution. They made enactments, and people took it seriously. The solution worked. Girls were able to get shidduchim once again, and a major social obstacle was overcome.

Fiction? No – Jewish Halachic history.

THE BACKGROUND

It was one of the enactments in a gathering called the Takanas Shum. The confluence of illness, danger and the crusades had contributed to the fact that there was a higher than normal mortality rate in the Jewish community. If a young woman's new groom were to pass away,

Chas v'shalom, the entire dowry that the bride came with – went to the husband's family. The bride's family did not get any of it back.

As a repercussion of this reality, many parents no longer provided their daughters with a large dowry. They did not wish to risk the significant sums of money that it entailed. As a consequence, the young girls sat single, with no prospects of shidduchim.

Something had to be done.

THE GEDOLIM GET TOGETHER

The great Gedolim of Medieval Europe, of the communities of Speyer Vermes and Mainz (forming the acronym Shum), gathered and made a number of takanos. Who were these great leaders? They were Rabbeinu Tam and the Rashbam, Rashi's grandsons. The Raavan, one of the early Baalei haTosfos. Over 250 Rabbis, Rishonim were in attendance.

THE SOLUTION TO THE SHIDDUCH CRISIS

The takanah that they made at the gathering was to decree that if a husband chas v'shalom passed away in the first year of marriage, the dowry would not be inherited by the husband's family, but it would revert back to the bride's parents. If he passed away within two years of marriage, then half of the dowry would go back to the bride's family (although this is a yesh omrim). The decree was passed and observed. The halacha is incorporated in the Shulchan Aruch and is mentioned in Even haEzer 53:3.

The gathering was held in the city of Troyes. It happened 857 years ago – in the year 1160.

But the result was that the Takanah worked. The parents of the brides began to once again give dowries and the young girls began to wed once again.

It solved the Shidduch crisis then.

WHAT WE NEED NOW

We need another Takanas Shum of sorts. We have girls that have not received shidduch calls in months – if not ever. This may be because of the disparity in numbers between available boys and girls, but whatever the reason may be – it needs to be resolved.

There are individual people and organizations that are attempting to address it. Reb Shlomo Yehudah Rechnitz tried to address it and even authored a number of articles and backed some initiatives too. But we need to make a macro-effort here.

This is something that should be on our spiritual agenda. If that Shidduch crisis of nearly 900 years ago so captured the attention of the Gedolei haRishonim, it is certainly be something that we should consider. The solution given then made it into the pages of our Shulchan Aruch. We need to address this issue on a grander scale.

Eavesdropping and Halacha

It is called "Operation Bugdrop" and it is causing entire countries to quake in fear. Essentially, this computer malware is virtually undetectable and can change any computer into an eavesdropping device. It records anything within earshot of the computer's built in mike. It was used to bring down the electric grid of the Ukraine. The malware was probably invented by Russia, but it was discovered by CyberX, the company founded by IDF cyber-security experts Omer Schneider and Nir Giller.

The fact that electronic eavesdropping is in the news, brings up the general question of whether or not eavesdropping in any form is halachically permitted. Two men are conversing about how a yeshiva is about to underwrite a construction initiative having nothing to do with education for profit-making purposes. Can one listen in? Two women are discussing zoning issues involving an indoor swimming pool. May one eavesdrop?

The Talmud and the Poskim in Shulchan Aruch discuss a concept called Hezek Ri'ya – damage caused by seeing. Yet neither the Talmud nor the Shulchan Aruch discuss a concept of damage of listening or eavesdropping. This may, at first glance, indicate to us that there is no inherent prohibition involved. Yet, we do find a debate about the issue in the writings of the Rishonim and acharonim.

THE TWO VIEWS IN THE MEFORSHIM

The Meiri (Beis HaBechira BB 2a) explains the issues of building a wall as resolving the concwpt of damage done by seeing into another's property. He states that there is no further issue of damage of eavesdropping by virtue of the thinness of the wall since people are generally careful in such matters and do not speak where it can be overheard.

Rav Eliyahu Mizrachi (1450-1526) in his responsum (#8) rules that there is no halachic issue of eavesdropping damage – since there is no mention of it in the Talmud.

According to the Meiri, when there is no reason for the person to think to be careful, such as with electronic eavesdropping, or by leaving his or her email open on the company computer – there would be a prohibition of eavesdropping.

REBBEINU GERSHOM

There is also the issue of the Cherem Rabbeinu Gershom (960-1040) not to read a letter of another person without him knowing. The Sefer Teshuvas Maharam (#1022) and the Be'er HaGolah (YD 334) cite the ban placed upon anyone who reads the letter of another person without that person's knowledge. It also states that if the recipient threw it out in the garbage, then one would be permitted to read it.

A pertinent question about this issue is as follows:

Does the Cherem Rabbeinu Gershom include eavesdropping on a conversation of others? Believe it or not there is a deep debate about this very issue among contemporary Poskim.

But even according to the view that it is not included in the ban, the underlying reasons of the ban still apply.

Rav Chaim Palagi in his Chokakei Lev explains the reasons for Rabbeinu Gershom's reason for the ban. One of his reasons is that it is a negation of v'ahavta l'rayacha kamocha – the Mitzvah of loving one's neighbor as oneself.

There is also the possible reason advanced by the Toras Chaim (347) that it is considered borrowing without permission (sho'el shelo midaas). However, not everyone agrees with this concept because the issue under discussion lacks physical form – it is information. That being the case, some would argue that it is not technical borrowing.

If we rule that the reason behind the ban is that it is an abnegation of the Torah Mitzvah of v'ahavta l'rayacha kamocha, the underlying reasons for Rabbeinu Gershom's ban still apply, so granted that he is not in violation of the Cherem – he is still in violation of the negation fo a Torah Mitzvah.

The Peleh Yoetz as well as Rav Palagi both explain that since one who reveals the secret obtained in a letter is in violation of a Lo Sa'aseh to reveal the secrets of others – "Lo Seilech Rachil B'Amecha – do not walk as a talebearer among your nation" there would be little difference as to how exactly he had obtained the information.

POSTCARDS, FAXES MEDICAL AND SCHOOL RECORDS

As an interesting side thought, the Shaivet HaKahasi (Vol. III #282) rules that the ban does apply to both postcards as well as faxes.

What else might be included in this prohibition? It seems that any information that a person would prefer to keep to himself or herself would also be included. Report card grades, regent marks, health and legal records, and even credit reports.

What about forwarding someone's email that was received and marked personal and confidential? Also, often there is a previous email that was attached in a chain or bundle to an item that you are forwarding now. May one read the bundle?

Many Poskim are of the opinion that an email is, in fact, included in Rabbeinu Gershom's ban. Regardless, although one may be curious, one should not look into the previous threads of an email that one has received if they were forwarded along with the current email that one legitimately received.

The Former VP's Son and the Other Daughter-in-law

The answer to everything lies in Torah.

And so, the Republicans who are criticizing former Vice president Joe Biden seem to be in agreement with a Rashi in Sanhedrin 58a. The Democrats who support Biden – they seem to be in agreement with the Ran and the Ramban's interpretation. Who would ever have imagined that an obscure debate in the Rishonim on how to interpret a passage of the Babylonian Talmudic tractate of Sanhedrin would have had such nationwide implications?

But let's start at the beginning.

Hallie Biden is the widow of Beau Biden, who was the son of the former vice president, Joe Biden. Beau Biden was also Delaware's attorney general before he passed away. Hallie Biden is now in a relationship with Beau's brother, Hunter. All this is according to the New York Post's Page Six.

Joe Biden and his wife Jill are supportive of the relationship. Hunter, Beau's brother, said to the Post, "Hallie and I are incredibly lucky to have found the love and support we have for each other in such a difficult time, and that's been obvious to the people who love us most." He further said, "We've been so lucky to have family and friends who have supported us every step of the way."

According to the Post, Hallie and Hunter began their relationship after the death of Hallie's husband of brain cancer in May 2015. The tragedy contributed to the decision of Joe Biden not to run for president.

Hunter is a 47-year-old lawyer. He is still married, but separated from his wife Kathleen. Hallie has two children.

The former vice-president and his wife remarked, "We are all lucky that Hunter and Hallie found each other as they were putting their lives together again after such sadness. They have mine and Jill's full and complete support and we are happy for them."

THE HALACHA

What is the halacha regarding such a relationship? Is Joe Biden's reaction acceptable according to Jewish law?

IF THEY WERE JEWISH

If everyone was Jewish, since Hallie and Beau had children, there would be a serious prohibition involved. If Hallie and Beau had no children, there would be a Mitzvah of Yibum (although not practiced nowadays) known as the Levarite Marriage involved. If they had children it would be a violation of the biblical prohibition of Aishes

Achiv. Hallie and Hunter's relationship would be considered one of Arayos – the forbidden relations. Any children from such a union would be considered Mamzerim.

DO GENTILES HAVE ARAYOS THROUGH MARRIAGE?

But they are not Jewish and the question is whether or not gentiles have Arayos that are created through marriage. This issue is a debate between two versions of Rabbi Meir, one according to his Rebbe, Rabbi Akiva and the other according to his Rebbe, Rabbi Eliezer in Sanhedrin 58a as to what was Rabbi Eleizer's view on the matter.

THE VIEW OF RABBI MEIR ACCORDING TO RABBI ELIEZER

This view held that gentiles are not commanded in the concept of forbidden arayos that have to do with marriage. Thus aside from the prohibition of adultery – according to Rabbi Meir's understanding of Rabbi Eliezer, for a gentile there is no further prohibition of a father's spouse or a brother's wife. Only blood-based arayos are forbidden according to Rabbi Meir's view.

THE VIEW OF RABBI AKIVA

Not so is the view of Rabbi Akiva acccording to Rabbi Meir. He holds that a father's spouse is forbidden to a gentile even after his father's death. Rabbi Akiva's halachic view, however, remains somewhat unclear. Does he hold that all of the relationships that develop through a marriage are considered arayos? Or does he just hold that it is true regarding a father's spouse but no one else?

DEBATE IN THE RISHONIM

The exact interpretation of Rabbi Akiva's view is a debate among the Rishonim. Rashi (1040-1105) is of the view that Rabbi Akiva considers all relationships that came about through a contracted marriage as part of the Arayos. Thus, according to Rashi's understanding of Rabbi Akiva – the relationship is illicit. But wait. The former VP can still rely on the Ran (1320-1376) on his comments in Sanhedrin and the Ramban (1194-1270) in his comments on Yevamos 98a. According to the Ramban, the fact that the father's wife is considered one of the Arayos is a special decree of the Torah, and cannot be extrapolated to the other Arayos.

OTHER HISTORICAL SIGNIFICANCE

This same debate between Rashi and the Ran and Ramban was the cause of the creation of the Anglican Church as well as the Episcopalian Church which broke away from the Anglican Church. If we recall our ninth grade European history, Henry VIII broke away from the Catholic Church and opened his own Church of England. But why? It was because he could not divorce his wife Catherine of Aragon. Pope Clement VII refused to annul his marriage or rather to rescind the special dispensation he had received from an earlier pope to allow his marriage to Catherine of Aragon.

Catherine had been previously married to Henry VIII's older brother Arthur. According to Henry VIII, she was forbidden to him. He held like Rashi, apparently. Pope Clement VII held that the marriage was valid and thus he would not annul it.

Henry the VIII then decided to form his own church – the Church of England. Eventually, Americans, who were members of the Anglican church had to form their own breakaway church – which they called the Episcopalian Church.

HOW COULD YAAKOV AVINU MARRY TWO SISTERS?

The Gemorah (Yuma 28b) tells us that the Avos fulfilled the Torah before it was given. This presents a question as to how Yaakov Avinu could have married two sisters, Rachel and Leah. Rav Yitzchok Zev Soloveitchik (in his Stencils on Torah SIman 5) uses this very same Ramban to answer this question. He writes that prior to Har Sinai, the nature of marriage was such that non-blood Arayos were not considered Arayos. L'havdil, Joe Biden's view is in accordance with the Brisker Rav.

THE BLESSINGS OF SHEVA BRACHOS

The Rosh in Kesuvos (Piskei HaRosh 1:12) asks a question: How can we say Vetzivanu al haArayos in the Sheva Brachos – gentiles also have arayos! Rav Velvel uses our Ramban to answer that it refers to the extra arayos that come about through marriage.

One can ask, however, this all makes sense according to the Ramban and the Ran. But what about Rashi? Rashi holds that a Ben Noach is also commanded in the marriage arayos. That being the case, how can we recite the blessing which seems to make it specifically a Jewish command?

A former student of mine, H.S., provided the following answer. Staying away from arayos is a force of Kedusha for Jews. It enables the Jewish people to reach a higher level of sanctity and closeness to G-d. That is why we read the parsha of Arayos from the Torah on Yom Kippur. The blessing is that the arayos sanctify us and that is unique to the Jewish nation – the ability to sanctify ourselves through staying away from the forbidden relations. This is. Lehavdil, also how the Republican detractors of Biden's reaction would also hold.

The Hat and Jacket for Davening

Here is the scenario:

Reuvain, who normally wears a hat and jacket for Tefilah, visits a client at a location with difficult parking. He has to bring along equipment into the client's office. Reuvain decides to leave his hat and jacket in the car. It is a scorcher. Shimon greets him and responds that he cannot meet with him now. Reuvain is early, and he, Shimon, is going to Mincha now.

Should Reuvain daven with Shimon without his hat and jacket? Or should he daven later with the proper dress?

THE SOURCES

The Gemorah in Shabbos 10a indicates that there is an obligation to wear a hat as one should daven in a manner that one greets a king. The halacha is codified in Shulchan Aruch Siman 91.

The language of the Shulchan Aruch is that chachomim and their students should dress like this. However, the Kaf HaChaim (91:26) writes that it applies to everyone.

The Sefer Chasidim #57 explains that the pasuk "Prepare to meet Hashem, Oh Israel" teaches us the obligation to dress properly before one davens in front of the King. Indeed, the Sefer Chassidim has strong words for those who only wear a hat on Shabbos.

The Mishna Brurah (91:12) writes that in our times, one must wear a hat for davening and a yarmulkah would not suffice, because it is not proper to stand in this manner in front of important people.

WHAT IF ONE WOULD MISS MINYAN ON ACCOUNT OF IT?

If he has no hat and jacket and if he were to wait until he received one he will miss davening with a minyan, Rav Shlomo Zalman Auerbach zt"l (Halichos Shlomo 2:15) ruled that the Mitzvah of Hechon – preparing oneself to stand before the King – does not set aside Tefillah b'Tzibbur. Likewise, Rav Yitzchok Zilberstein Shlita ruled that he should daven without the hat and jacket (Chashukei Chemed Bechoros 44b).

However, Rav Zilberstein qualifies this ruling as only when it was on account of an accident. But one who purposefully goes somewhere and he know that he will have to daven but does not take along his hat and jacket, he should not daven. The reason is that he is showing that he is mezalzel in the honor of Hashem. Rav Zilberstein explains that this was also the position of Rav Elyashiv zt"l.

DOES IT STILL APPLY IN THE POST KENNEDY WORLD?

In the twenties, thirties, forties, fifties and early sixties – everyone wore a hat. It is a debate as whether or not it was President Kennedy whose example as president caused the nation to stop wearing hats or whether it was just non-conformity in the 1960's and he was just part of it (See Neil Steinberg's book Hatless Jack: the President, the Fedora, and the History of American Style). In other words, was President Kennedy a siman or a siba? Regardless, nowadays people have stopped wearing hats.

Some people therefore argue that the Mishna Brurah only applies when people wear formal dress. However, in modern times, no one greets the president of the United States while wearing a hat – so this would no longer apply. One of my Rebbeim zt"l counter-argued that if there was a law that one must keep their head covered, no one would be using a yarmulkah to fulfill this law. Since we do have such a law, it is proper to perform it while wearing a hat.

IT WAS THE COMMUNISTS

Rav Moshe Shternbuch (Teshuvos v'hanhagos Vol. IV #26) argues that even though in Israel it is common practice to stand before important people without a hat and jacket – this is irrelevant. He explains that they learned this practice from the other nations of the world who picked up the practice from the Communists. It is a communist ideal of everyone being absolutely equal that gave birth to the idea that one does not need to dress formally in front of important people.

There is another aspect that one must dress like a Ben Torah. Indeed, the Talmud in Brachos 6b tells us that Rabbi Yehudah would take care to ensure that he was always dressed fittingly before davening.

GETTING BACK TO OUR CASE

If Reuvain could have davened later in a minyan with a hat and jacket (and he normally does so) then it would seem that he should daven later. Although there is a concept called Zrizin Makdimin l'mitzvos, people who are fastidious jump to perform Mitzvos early, we do not see that this sets aside the Mitzvah of davening in proper attire.

Rectifying Karais

A wealthy philanthropist in shul, about to turn sixty, had just scheduled a colonoscopy. Interestingly enough, he had scheduled the test not because his doctor recommended it, but rather because he was about to turn sixty. His concern is that he wants to make sure that he has not incurred the penalty of Kareis – the penalty of being cut-off.

Presumably, his actions were based upon the Gemorah in Moed Katan (28a) where Rav Yoseph made a party upon reaching the age of sixty because he made it to sixty and therefore did not incur the punishment of Kareis. Abaye pointed out that there is a second type of Kareis called Kareis of days. Rav Yoseph replied that just outliving Kareis of years is also a reason to celebrate.

It is an unfortunate reality that there are many nice people out there who may have something rather serious hanging over them. That something is the Divine punishment known as kareis—being cut off. This penalty is associated with a number of violations: desecrating Shabbos, improper relationships. eating blood, breaching the prohibition of niddah, eating on Yom Kippur, eating cheilev, going onto prohibited places on Har HaBayis...the list goes on.

THE QUESTION

Kareis, of course, is quite serious. But can anything be done? Is there a means by which kareis can be rectified? If so, how? And why haven't we heard about it before? Is there a particularly propitious time for it?

The answer to this question, fortunately, is "yes." With the Yom Tov of Shavuos quickly approaching, however, there is now a possibility of double-dipping. But, there are other requirements.

LEARNING ALL NIGHT

The great AriZal, Rabbi Yitzchak Luria (Shaar Ruach HaKodesh, p. 11b) describes a rectification ritual known as tikkun kareis. He writes as follows: "One who is awake all night and does not sleep at all, and immerses himself in the study of Torah that entire night will exempt himself from one punishment of kareis if, Heaven forbid, he has incurred it. Each night exempts one kareis."

So here we have it. One night of all night-learning can rectify one violation of Kareis.

THE THOUGHT PROCESS

Rav Chaim Vital, the foremost student of the AriZal, adds more information about the exact kavanos – intentions that one must have while learning Torah for the rectification: One must connect his neshamah to the root above, thus rectifying Adam Elyon. Practically, this means that he should focus and picture his neshama connecting and originally emanating from the upper heavenly sphere.

THE FOUR CAVEATS

Other caveats that Rav Chaim Vital adds are to refrain from 1] haughtiness, 2] anger, 3] being makpid — being overly-strict with people, and 4] lashon ha'ra. It is, of course, worthwhile to study an overview of each of these midos and actions to ensure that one does not violate them.

WHAT TO STUDY

Rav Alexander Ziskind of Grodno (d. 1794) author of the Sefer Yesod VeShoresh HaAvodah (Shaar HaKollel) adds to this. He writes that it is proper to study a subject that is related to the sin that one has committed, and that there are some propitious times for this ritual. The two most propitious times are during Yamim Nora'im and during the weeks of Shovevim Tat.

What is "Shovevim Tat"? It is a special time when teshuvah is more effective: the weeks that we read Sh'mos, Va'eira, Bo, BeShallach, Yisro, Mishpatim, Terumah, and Tetzaveh. The names of these parashios form the acronym "Shovevim Tat," which means "those who return." He also adds that, ideally, one should perform this tikkun while standing.

WHO ELSE DISCUSSES IT

Does anyone else discuss this tikkun? Do any of the standard rabbinical texts and sources reference it? Are there any any Litvishe— non-Chassidish and non-Sephardic gedolim—who discuss it?

The answer is yes. The Chofetz Chaim discusses it. But first some background:

The Rif (Rabbi Yitzchok Alfasi) is known for his commentary summarizing the more pertinent aspects of the Talmud for us. The problem is that he did not write such a work on the order of the Talmud known as Kodshim. To help fill this lacuna, the Chofetz Chaim himself wrote such a work, called Likutei Halachos. In the beginning of Maseches Kerisus the Chofetz Chaim references this custom cited in the Kabbalistic texts of Tikkun Kareis,

SOMETHING ELSE TO STUDY

The Chofetz Chaim adds the following words after he discusses the minhag of Tikkun Kareis: "It is certain that if a person learns the entire maseches that deals with the punishment of kareis and the ways to avoid it, it will be enormously effective in cleansing his neshamah." He further adds that it is especially true if he knows it well. There are 28 pages in Kerisus (and it is only one volume in the ArtScroll), so it should not be stupendously difficult to master.

A LIST OF FASTS

The AriZal also provides a list of sins with a corresponding number of fasts that will atone for those sins (also in Shaar Ruach HaKodesh). The commentators ask (see Ohr LeTzion Vol. III, Ch. 30) an interesting question: Do these fasts atone for every instance of that particular sin, or is the entire cadre of fasts listed necessary for each and every instance of violation of each sin? Or perhaps is there a sort of "all-day pass" that requires more fasts, but not the entire list for each violation?

It seems that the answer to this question is cause for debate among halachic (or kabbalistic-halachic) authorities. The first Lubavitcher Rebbe, Rabbi Shneur Zalman of Liady, writes in chapter three of his Iggeres HaTeshuvah (found in the Tanya) that it is necessary to fast three times the amount listed in the AriZal's list, and the entire aveirah is thus fully atoned for. Rav Yoseph Chaim in response Rav Pealim (Vol.

III, No. 35) writes that one only need follow the AriZal's formula once, and each violation of that sin in the past is atoned for.

REDEEMING FASTS WITH TZEDAKAH

There is also an accepted practice to redeem the fasts with tzedakah. This practice is cited by the Mishnah Berurah, the GraZ, and the Kaf HaChaim (O.C. 119:15). To calculate the proper amount, one must figure out the portion cost per meal (for that day) and multiply it by the numbers listed by the AriZal. He also points out that one cannot mix tikkunim; each fasting for a particular sin must be kept separate.

ONLY AFTER AGE TWENTY

The punishment of kareis is only for prohibitions one committed after the age of 20. So even though one is certainly liable for sins committed at age 13–20 (12–20 for girls), the punishment of kareis does not begin until one's 20th birthday. Some authorities read the Rambam as being of the opinion that liability for kareis begins at 13; they infer this from what he writes in the laws of milah, that from age 13 if one did not yet have a b'ris milah he must do so, and if he does not, he is chayav kareis. However, the Rambam clearly writes in his commentary to the seventh chapter of Sanhedrin that the period for kareis begins at age 20.

NO PREREQUISITE OF WARNING

To be liable for kareis, there is no prerequisite of hasra'ah (warning). The reason is that since the punishment is meted out by Heaven, it is clearly known in the heavenly courts what the perpetrators intentions were.

CONCLUSION

In conclusion, we see that there are steps by which one can recover from a kareis violation. They involve sincere repentance, special kavanos, and all-night Torah study. Ultimately, it is worthwhile to pursue, since Hashem does not want the death or destruction of those who sin. Rather, He desires our penance and return to Torah and His ways. The Yom Tov of Shavuos is coming up and it gives people an opportunity to learn all night. We should take advantage of it.

Lighting a Yartzeit Candle

It is the custom within Klal Yisroel to light a Yartzeit candle on the day that a relative had passed away. The lighting has no accompanying blessing, and people would like to express themselves in a Tefillah when lighting the candle. This is not only true on a Yartzeit but whenever Yom Tov comes as well.

The author of the Peleh Yoetz, Rabbi Eliezer Papo (1785–1828), did in fact compose such a prayer. Rav Papo was the Rabbi of the city of Selestria in Bulgaria. Bulgaria was a part of the Ottoman Empire at the time. The Tefillah of the Pelehe Yoetz is reproduced and translated below, as a public service.

תפילה הנמצאת בספר אלף המגן מבעל הפלא יועץ על פרשת ויצא עמוד כ"ד

הריני מדליק נר זה למנוחת ולעילוי נשמת אבי מורי _____ בן _____

יהי רצון מלפניך ה' אלקינו ואלהי אבותינו, שתקבל ברחמים וברצון כל מעשה הטוב שאני עושה, בין במחשבה, בין בדיבור, בין במעשה ויהיה הכל לזכות ולמנוחת ולעילוי לנשמות עמך ישראל, ובפרט לנפש רוח ונשמה של אמי _____ . יהי רצון שתהינה נפשותיהם צרורות בצרור החיים.

Behold I am lighting this lamp for the resting and uplifting of the soul of my father, my teacher _____ the son of _____.

May it be Your will before you, Hashem our G-d and the G-d of our forefathers, that all my good deeds whether in thought, speech or action be done for a merit and a resting and an elevation of the souls of your nation Israel. It should be especially for the soul of my mother _____. May it be Your will that their souls be bound in the pebbles of life.

Is Pink – Halachically Considered to be Red?

They appear not only in the headlines of New York City newspapers, but in New York City courthouses. They are two female Orthodox Jewish criminal lawyers, one 40 and one 26, that happen to wear bright pink outfits – even down to their matching Chanel patent leather pink flats. They call themselves, "Double Trouble" and by numerous accounts they are a formidable team. One of them was quoted by the paper as stating, "We comply with Orthodox Jewish rules of modesty, but we like to wear pink."

It is this last statement to which this article is addressed. Hopefully, the two lawyers will respond positively to this halachic analysis (and not with a lawsuit). Their names are _____ and _____ (we will see if the Five Towns Jewish Times lawyers allow their names to be mentioned in this article). But first the background.

[For those interested in the original article, see http://www.nydailynews.com/new-york/double-trouble-law-partners-wear-pink-outfits-court-article-1.3002790]

THE BACKGROUND

The Gemorah in Brachos 20a tells us of the self-sacrifice of Rabbi Adda Bar Ahava who encountered what appeared to be a Jewish woman wearing a "karbalusah" in the market place (red scarf). He took it away from her and the woman subsequently took Rav Adda Bar Ahava to court. He lost and had to pay the rather large sum of 400 zuz. He inquired what her name was and when she responded, "Matun" – he responded: "If only I had listened to your name: Matun (translation: be patient), I would have saved myself 400 zuz."

The Ben Yehoyadah asks why this particular incident constitutes mesiras nefesh or self-sacrifice. He answers that Rav Adda bar Ahavah was unsure as to whether or not she was a Jewish woman or not and felt that it was worth the risk to ensure that a Jewish girl not violate a prohibition.

WHY DID HE RIP IT?

The Aruch and the approach of most commentaries is that Rav Adda bar Ahava ripped the article of clothing on account of its apparent lack of modesty in color (it was an overgarment over other clothing – something like a sign post). The Maharal (Netzach Yisroel chapter 25) understands that he ripped it on account of it being an article that Jews shouldn't wear on account of it being like the gentiles. In other words the Maharal does not understand the ripping as being on account of it being immodest but because of assimilation.

FIVE APPROACHES

Regardless as to what the self-sacrifice actually was and why it was ripped, there seem to be four approaches in the commentaries as to what exactly the prohibition would have been in a Jewish girl wearing a karbalusah.

FIRST APPROACH

The Aruch and Tosfos in Kesuvos 72a explain that it is pritzus – a breach of decency and brings to sin. The Shach (YD 178:3) further explains in the name of the Maharik (Shoresh 88) that it is not the manner of modest people to go in red, and that this is a tradition in the hands of the Jewish people. It is not the manner of tzniyus and hachna'ah – a humility of dress.

SECOND APPROACH

In Teshuvos Binyomin Z'eev Vol. II # 282 "v'kaivan d'hacha" he explains that red is very important and exotic in a sense, and it is not the way of Jewish women to dress in such a manner. Many understand this as complementing the idea of hachna'ah, humility of dress, expressed above.

THIRD APPROACH

The Nemukei Yoseph seems to provide a third explanation that red is the color used by the priests of Avodah Zarah and that in wearing red, there is a trace of violating Avodah Zarah.

FOURTH APPROACH

The fifth approach is that of the Teshuvos Gaonim Kadmonim (#101) who write that he perceived that this article of clothing contained Shaatnez (Klaim) – a prohibited mixture of fibers. Indeed, this is also the approach of the Trumas haDeshen (Siman 276).

FIFTH APPROACH

The Chasam Sofer has a different approach that the power of Aisav stemmed from red- or Mars. He cites the interpretation of Rabbeinu Bachya on the verse, "Halitaini nah min haAdom hazeh – feed me from this red" – and that is something entirely foreign to and unbecoming of the Jewish nation.

PLUGGING IT ALL BACK IN

There may be a second or corollary issue of Tznius (modesty) in bringing excessive attention to oneself, but for now, we are dealing with the particular issue of wearing red. Starting from the last explanation backward – according to the Chasam Sofer – pink would not be an issue since this hardly evokes the red of Mars or Aisav. Nor would the lawyers' attire bring up a problem of a specific problem of Shaatnez. Pink was not used in Avodah Zarah, so that would address issue number three. There is also nothing particularly super-important about pink that would make it extremely exotic. The only issue is that of the first one – modesty. This is the view, however, that the Shulchan Aruch seems to adopt.

GUIDELINES FOR RED

The halacha is that the item must either be entirely red or the majority of it visibly red (see 178:1 and commentaries). Rav Elyashiv zt"l had ruled (see Halichos Bas Yisroel p. 92 footnote 7b) the color Bordeaux is not considered red for these purposes. The author extends that to other types of off-red as well.

The origin of the word Karbalusa is explained by both Rabbeinu Chananel and the Aruch as referencing the fleshy red part on top of a rooster or chicken's head. This would seem to be the type of red that is referenced in the Gemorah.

THE OTHER VIEW

Rav Moshe Shternbuch (Teshuvos v'Hanhagos Vol. I #136) Shlita seems to understand the aforementioned Gemorah that it includes any color that brings attention to oneself. Thus, a bright yellow or bright pink would be included in the prohibition according to Rav Shternbuch. Rav Chaim Kanievsky is also quoted as forbidding any bright color. Other Poskim cite other sources for not bringing excess attention to oneself and forbid any bright or neon color. They do not state that their source is this Gemorah in Brachos, however.

THOSE WHO ARE LENIENT REGARDING RED

In Sefer Mitzvos HaBayis Vol. II page 145, a ruling issued by Rav Yitzchok Elchanan Spector is cited that states, "nowadays gentile women no longer wear red as a sign of pritzus – the Gemorah is no longer applicable." This view was originally published in a 1800's Torah journal. Clearly, however, Rav Elyashiv and other more contemporary Poskim do not adopt the approach of Rav Yitzchok Elchonon.

Morning Coffee in the Wrong Place

Many people have argued about Dunkin Coffee versus Starbucks. It is a battle between the two brands. Some like Starbucks because it is stronger. Others like Dunkin's because it is sweeter.

There is a war between their business models too. Dunkin stores are mostly franchises. Starbucks are mostly corporate owned. Who is winning the war? Starbucks has 22,519 stores – Dunkin only 11,500. Starbucks made 16.8 billion dollars last year, Dunkin only 828.9 million.

But this war is not between the two brands. It is between the Shul Gabbaim and both of the brands. This is because of late, many people have been bringing their coffee not only into shul but into davening itself.

They say brachos and have the first intra-davening sip. Before Boruch sh'amar is the second sip. The third sip comes at ashrei. The cup of Joe is half gone by birchas Krias Shma. If it is a latte, then it is half gone only by Ezras Avosainu.

What is the halacha here? Is this permitted? What about if a person is weak or simply cannot function without coffee – would it be permitted for him?

THE FOUR CUPS OF WINE ON PESACH

Perhaps we can find the answer to our question with another question. How come we make four blessings over wine at the Pesach seder? Why are the four cups not covered with one bracha?

Rav Amram Gaon (800? to 875) answers this question in his siddur, and one of his answers is as follows: "Similarly, a group of people celebrating who were seated and established drinking over wine, and got up to pray and prayed. They subsequently returned to drink – they must recite a Borei Pri HaGafen. Why must they do so? They did not remove themselves from that place?

Rather, since they arose to pray and they may not drink during prayer – it is considered like they interrupted and they must recite the blessing [again]. So too, here. Since he recited the Hagaddah and he may not drink during the hagaddah, it is as if he has interrupted and he must recite the blessing. Because of these reasons each of the cups necessitates its own blessing"

One can see clearly from Rav Amram gaon's words that not only is it forbidden to drink during the Shmoneh Esreh, but even during the other parts of davening. There is no substantive difference between the Hagaddah and davening, and the fact that Rav Amram Gaon compares the two indicates clearly that drinking coffee during Davening is forbidden.

EATING BEFORE DAVENING

There is also a halacha that it is forbidden to eat before davening. This is based upon a Gemorah in Brachos (10b) and is codified in Shulchan Aruch (89:3). It is considered haughty to take care of one's own needs before tending to our obligations toward Hashem. A drink is permitted, according to the Mishna Brurah (89:22). Nowadays, it is even permitted to add sugar and milk to one's coffee, but breakfast before davening, is forbidden unless one is weak or sic k(See Minchas Yitzchok Vol. IV #28).

This entire discussion, however, is only for eating and drinking before davening – but no one ever even contemplated the issue during Davening. That is why, the issue is not even touched upon in the Poskim despite the fact that coffee has been around for many centuries.

THE ISSUE OF DOING IT IN SHUL

There is another issue and that is eating and drinking in shul. The Shulchan Aruch 151:1 writes:

"Our shuls and Batei Midrashim, we are not to conduct ourselves within them light-headed activity such as laughter and humor and extraneous conversation. Nor do we eat and drink in them.."

The Sefer Yereim (Amud HaKorbanos page 386) brings two explanations for the prohibition of eating or drinking in a shul. One reason is on account of Moreh Mikdash – having the proper awe and reverence for the House of Hashem. The second reason is on account of Me'ilah b'hekdesh – the misuse of Hekdesh. The Bais HaKnesses is singled out as a special place devoted exclusively to Hashem. Eating and drinking inside the shul would be a negation of this. Although some shuls are built with the permission to eat and drink at a Kiddush afterward, in no way did they originally have in mind that one may eat during actual prayers.

It is clear from the verses in Vayikra 26:31 that shuls are considered a Mikdash. It is for this reason that shuls are exempt from the Mitzvah of Mezuzah (See Rambam hilchos Tefillah 6:6).

Of course, if a person is truly sick and requires the coffee in order to become healed – then he may drink and eat as necessary. However, there is another issue. People who observe him are unaware that he is sick, and there may also be a Maris Ayin issue where people might think that such behavior is, in fact permitted for healthy people as well.

CHILLUL HASHEM

Finally, there is one last issue and that is the concept of Chillul Hashem. Gentiles are quite careful neither to eat nor drink while in a church. Is it not a grave desecration of Hashem's Name that we, the Jewish people, drink while standing in prayer before the King of all kings? Lest the reader question this last point, Rav Dovid Tzvi Hoffman zt"l (in his Melamed l'Ho'il Orech Chaim Siman 15) cites this very same issue in regard to smoking within a shul. He brings up the idea that gentiles do not smoke in their churches. How then can we do so ourselves?

It is clear from all of the above that we should stop this practice immediately. Whether the coffee is from Starbucks, Dunkin, home-brewed or from any other place – the shul should not be a coffee house. We must also keep in mind that America, indeed, the world runs not on Dunkin' but on Tefillah. It is, as it states in Pirkei Avos, one of the three pillars that hold up the world. In the merit of our davening and treating our shuls and our Tefilos with the greatest of respect – may we merit Moshiach Tzidkeinu bimheira b'yameinu, amain!

Reasons for the Brachos

Generally speaking, there are four reason why the sages initiated the blessings.

1. To thank G-d for the specific item from which one is benefitting. Otherwise, it would be considered as a form of theft.

2. To develop ourselves into Baalei Hakaras HaTov – people that recognize that which others do for us. The Neviim have taught us of the greatest ideals: love, brotherhood, gratitude. However, these thoughts and ideals do not come about instantly as if by magic. They come through many years of hard work. It is no different than a piano player or karate expert. The brachos change us into people who appreciate that which is done for us.

3. To ensure that no matter what we are involved in, we will always be thinking about Hashem — about things far beyond our own small world.

4. To help us develop a unique bond with Hashem called, "Dveikus." In this bond we attempt to emulate Hashem as well.

BLESSINGS

Bentching after we eat bread is Torah in origin, provided that we ate until we were satisfied. By Rabbinic decree, even if we ate a mere kezayis of bread — we still must bentch. The Rabbis who established the other blessings were Ezra and his Bais Din. They are called the "Anshei Knesses HaGedolah – the Men of the Great Assembly."

They enacted that every blessing must contain something called "Shaim" and "Malchus." Shaim is Hashem's Great name. malchus is the mention of His great Kingdon.

ONE HUNDRED BLESSINGS A DAY

Dovid HaMelech was experiencing a terrible national calamity wherein one hundred people were dying of a plague each day. He discerned that there was lack of Yiras Shamayim, of fear of Heaven. In order to address this problem, he ordained that it was necessary to recite 100 blessings each day. After this was ordained, the plague had stopped. Who is obligated in reciting these 100 blessings? Rav Wolbe zt"l, author of the Alei Shor, writes that women are exempt. He writes that, generally speaking, women have a naturally high level of fear of Heaven.

The Gemorah (Menachos 43b) tells us that the obligation is alluded to in a pasuk in Dvarim (10:12), "V'atta Yisroel, mah Hashem Elokecha sho'el m'imcha" – do not read mah, but read it as me'ah – one hundred.

Rav 'Bun said that in the future each person is going to have to give an account and reckoning on that which his eyes saw, but he did not eat of.

BRACHA LEVATALA

There is a prohibition to recite something called a Bracha Sh'aina tzricha. There is something that we can call "word evolution" – that is words can take on different meanings and connotations over time. When the Gemorah discusses Bracha sh'aina tzricha it refers to something that we now call a bracha levatalah. A bracha levatalah is a bracha that is COMPLETELY in vain. In other words, it should not be said. Indeed, the Gemorah tells us that whomsoever recites it, it is as if he has violated taking the Name of Hashem in vain.

There seems to be a debate as to whether or not this statement is meant to be taken literally or not. Many Poskim (Mishna Brurah, Mogain Avrohom) understand the Rambam as being of the opinion that a bracha levatalah is actually a Torah prohibition. Tosfos, however, explain that it is a Rabbinic violation. Why was it couched in such a serious terms? In order to emphasize to us how serious we should take it.

Some Poskim (Chazon Ish) suggest that even the Rambam might hold that it is not a biblical prohibition, but rather Rabbinic. Why then does he write that it is biblical? They answer that it is for the same reason that the Gemorah did – to teach us how far we should stay away from it.

BRACHA SH'AINA TZRICHA

There is also, something that we now call a Bracha Sh'aina Tzricha and that is having caused an unnecessary bracha. There are a few examples of this:

1.   If someone has fruits in front of him, all of the same blessing, and the person specifically excludes some of the fruits and recites another blessing on those that he excluded.

2.   Reciting a bracha achrona, terminating the eating session, and thus having to recite another blessing again.

3.   Changing one's place in a manner that another blessing must be recited.

4.   Eating foods of the meal before one has washed.

FIXING A BRACHA LEVATALA

When a bracha levatalah was recited, it is necessary to repair it by saying, "Borcuh Shaim Kvod Malchuso l'olam vo'aid." This is true even if one merely says the shaim Hashem inappropriately. Indeed, Gedolim have ruled that it must still be said even if one said the shaim hashem in another language. Oh Em _____, is an example.

If one had just said the words, "Boruch atta hashem" he should append the words, "Lamdeini chukecha – which is a pasuk in Tehillim (119:10). Thus he ended up not having said a bracha levatalah.

If he had already pronounced the first three syllables of the next shaim hashem – "elokai" but did not pronounce the fourth syllable of "nu" he should complete it with the words, "Yisroel avinu m'olam v'ad olam." This would make it a pasuk in Divrei HaYamim I (29:1). The problem is that, it is only the latter half of that pasuk. It begins with the words , "And Dovid haMelech blessed and said:" Therefore, although it may help to reduce the impact of the bracha levatalah, we still recite, "boruch shaim kevod malchuso l'olam vo'ed" afterward.

TOCH KEDAI DIBBUR – HOW LONG?

If one recited an incorrect blessing which would not be effective for that food, it can be corrected if one changes his wording in the time frame called, "toch kedai dibbur." How long is "toch kedai dibbur?" It is the time that it takes to say (See MB 206:10), "Shalom Alecha Rebbe." There is a bit of a contradiction in the Mishna Brurah, however. Elsewhere (267:9), he writes that it is the time it takes to say, "Shalom Alecha Rebbe umori." Most Poskim go with the three word time frame, rather than the four word one. In this author's experience and experiments, the three word time frame ranges from 1.11 to 1.49 seconds. The "umori" would add .4 of a second.

One of my Rebbeim had posed the following question to Rav Shlomo Zalman Auerbach zt"l. Does use, of "uh, uh, uh" extend the time frame of "toch k'dai dibbur?" He responded, in fact, that it does. "This can go on, almost indefinitely," responded Rav Shlomo Zalman.

The Blessing for Kings

The election of President Trump, and the presence of a Shomer Shabbos daughter and son-in-law, has sparked new interest in the blessing that is recited upon kings. Indeed, the issue even made it into the Annual Five Towns Brachos contest. Does we recite a blessing over President Trump? Is it just kings who have life or death in their hands, or is it even U.S. presidents?

The Shulchan Aruch (OC 324:8) rules that on Jewish kings one recites the blessing, Boruch atta Hashem, elokainu melech ha'olam – sh'chalak mikvodo lirayav. On kings of the nations of the world one recites the blessing, "boruch sh'nasan mikvodo l'basar vadam." This is based upon a passage in Brachos 58a. The blessing, it seems, is recited with Shaim uMalchus – mentioning the Name of G-d as well as mentioning His Kingship over the wolrd.

HOW OFTEN

But how often is this blessing recited? What if you happen to be Jared and Ivanka? Do you say it every day? It would seem that the blessing is only made once in every thirty days, according to a quote of the Raavad found in the Orchos Chaim. It is also interesting to note that in the Sefer Chasidim (#950) there is a limitation placed on this Mitzvah. It seems that if one never saw the king (or president) then one should try to go see him. If, however, he had already seen him, the Sefer Chassidim writes, then he should not be mevatel from his Torah studies.

IF IVANKA RUNS..

What happens if, in the future, Ivanka Kushner, the president's popular daughter, chooses to run and wins? Which version of the blessing would be recited – the first version for Jewish kings or the second version for kings of the nations? The Sho'el v'nishal (OC Vol. I #73) rules that if that person were to follow the ways of the Torah than the first version is recited. Otherwise it would be the second version.

PRESIDENT TRUMP IN PLAIN CLOTHES

What would be the halacha if the president were to forgo high-end clothing and were to try and go incognito – such as in overalls? The Kaf haChaim 324:33 cites numerous Poskim who state that the blessing was only enacted when the physical manifestations of that Kavod are present. The Halacha Brurah (Vol. XI p. 305), Rav Ovadiah Yosef's son, rules that one does not recite the blessing in such a situation with Shaim uMalchus – but just the words themselves. Ashkenazic Poskim do not cite this caveat. One should check with one's own Rav or Posaik.

DOES HE HAVE TO SEE HIM?

The Debreciner Rav rules that if one saw the president on television the blessing is not said. Indeed, one does not even say it without shaim uMalchus.

Rav Dovid Yosef write that one does not actually have to witness the president or king. Even if one was just able to see his entourage and knew that he was there, that would be sufficient. It is for this reason that even a blind person may recite this blessing when he feels that the president is present. If he does not actually feel it, but is merely told that the president is here, then he does not recite the blessing (p. 308).

ARE PRESIDENTS LIKE KINGS?

Rav Ovadia Yosef zt"l ruled (Yechave Daas 2:28) that the blessing is recited as long as the person in charge can either execute or pardon someone from exection. He cites the Radvaz (Vol. I #296) as well as the Orchos Chaim (Hilchos Brachos Siman 49) to this effect.

Rav Dovid Yosef Shlita in his Halacha Brurah (Vol. XI page 306) writes that one recites the blessing with Shaim UMalchus even on a democratically elected leader of a limited term. This is true only as long as his pardoning cannot be overruled.

What about a President who doesn't wear royal clothing? Rav Ovadia Yosef zt"l in his Yabia Omer 8:22:25) writes that when the President Richard Nixon flew to Israel the blessing was recited without Shaim u'Malchus. It seems, however, that this concept has evolved a bit, taking into account that in Western countries, kings and leaders just don't wear royal clothing anymore. Thus, Rav Dovid Yosef rules that even if the king is not wearing specialized clothing but is wearing respectable clothing and is surrounded by other significant people, then a blessing is made with Shaim uMalchus.

Rav Vosner is Shaivet haLevi I #35 rules that shaim uMalcus is recited on the president. The Debreciner Rav ruled (Be'er Moshe Vol. II #9) that shaim uMalchus is not recited. Rav Moshe Shternbuch (Teshuvos V'hanhagos Vol. II #139 rules that the temporary nature of the presidency is what would disqualify it from the shaim uMalchus aspect of the blessing.

THE REASONS

The Gemorah explains that one should actually make an effort to see kings in order to be able to distinguish between Jewish and non-Jewish kings. Rashi explains that the reference is to Melech haMashiach, when he arrives. Seemingly, the reason is so that we can better appreciate Moshiach – when he finally arrives, and the Chessed that Hashem has done for us.

The Rambam seems to imply a different reason. The Gemorah (Megillah 15b) tells us that Esther was punished when she went to see Achashveirosh and she reached the outer hall. The Shechina was no longer with her and she noticed the deficit and recited the verse in Tehillim (22), "Hashem, Hashem, why have You abandoned me?" One of the questions of self-examination that she asked herself was that perhaps she had incorrectly referred to Achashveirosh disparagingly. She then immediately corrected herself. The Rambam explains in his commentary to Esther (5:1) that Hashem had given of His Kavod to flesh and blood and it was wrong of her to speak of him in a pejorative manner. It seems from this Rambam, the reason for the bracha is to take note of the honor which Hashem endowed a human being.

TO AMALEK

It is interesting to note that in the early 20th century, when Kaiser Wilhelm came to Yerushalayim on a Shabbos, the 13th of Cheshvan in 5659, they told Rav Yoseph Chaim Sonnenfeld zt"l of his imminent arrival. He was to arrive at 3:00 PM. Yet the Rav did not wish to greet him. They inquired as to why not. He responded that he had a tradition from the Vilna Gaon that the German people were safaik Amalek and that it is forbidden to recite the blessing of, "boruch shenasan mikvodo l'basar vadam." One of my Rebbeim, a holocaust survivor, had related this incident to me some thirty five years ago and wondered, "In light of the holocaust, it may no longer be a safaik."

Why Poppy Seeds?

Now that the month of Adar has arrived, people will have started to make their Hamantaschen. Traditionally, hamantaschen have been made out of poppy seeds, although, of late, there are all sorts of other fillers that have popped up. Why poppy seeds?

The minhag was based upon a Ramah in Shulchan Aruch, where he cites the Kol Bo and writes (OC 695:2), "Some say that it is a custom to eat zironim – seeds on Purim, as a commemoration of the seeds that Daniel and his friends ate in Babylonia."

Both the Pri Chadash and the Aruch haShulchan (OC 695:9) pose the following question:

Daniel? This is Purim – about Esther, not Daniel! Also, the Gemorah (Megillah 13a) tells us that Esther also ate seeds when she first came to the palace – Haigai fed it to her. Why then does the Ramah only quote Daniel?

Also, the Mishna Brurah mentions the Gemorah too, but does not address the question of the Pri Chadash and the Aruch haShulchan.

I would like to propose the following answer.

Esther knew that there was rhyme and reason to her being taken into the palace. She knew that she was in need of a miracle. And now, those in charge of the women who were brought to the palace were offering them anything. She could have had her choice of any kosher food. Why then did she pick seeds?

Esther most certainly was aware of the miracle that happened to Daniel and his friends in the very beginning of Sefer Daniel. After ten days they were healthier and finer than all the others solely on a diet of seeds. This was the beginning of the help that Daniel rendered to his people. Perhaps she should take the same avenue.

With this answer we have greater insight into the minhag of eating poppy seed hamantaschen. Just as there was a miracle that occurred to Klal Yisroel regarding the seeds that Daniel and his friends ate, wherein they adhered strictly to the Kosher dietary laws through seeds and just like Esther tried to follow in those footsteps, so too should we merit miracles by virtue of our adhering carefully to the Torah's dietary laws as symbolized by the poppy seeds.

There is another message about Purim that everyone could gain from. Daniel merited a miracle by keeping kosher. Esther did too. This is the reason behind our custom of eating poppy hamantaschen. Isn't it time that every Jew who eats a Hamantashchen look into keeping kosher too?

Matanos L'Evyonim

One of the Mitzvos of Purim is that there is a mitzvah to give at least one gift to two different poor people on Purim day. Even a poor person who himself has reached a financial state that he must ask for charity, must still give.

What if a person gives to a poor person and his son who is supported by his father? Would this be considered as if he has given to one person or to two people? The Aruch HaShulchan (OC 694:2) is of the opinion that it is only considered as if he has given to one person. Rav Forsheimer, however, point to the Maharsha (Megillah 7b "shedar') which indicates that it is considered as two people.

This obligation may be fulfilled through any type of gift — money, food, drink, or clothing. One should, however, try to give a substantial monetary gift. If one does use money, ideally it should be enough to buy bread weighing at least three eggs — five slices, approximately. At the very least, however, one must give a perutah (now 3 cents) or its equivalent value to each of two poor persons. A perutah is 1/1244th of an ounce of silver.

Rav Shmuel Kamenetsky, shlita, rules that the minimum amount should be $1. The Shaarei Teshuvah rules that it should be the equivalent amount of the cost of a meal for a poor person. In modern times this amounts to approximately five dollars (Rav Shmuel Fuerst.) .

These gifts should be given in the daytime, after the Megillah is read. Matanos la'evyonim should be above and beyond maaser.

Money set aside for matanos la'evyonim should not be changed to another tzedakah without a ruling from a posek.

One is not overly strict with the poor on Purim to determine whether they are really poor or not. Whoever puts his hand out — we give him. According to leading poskim, this does not apply to organizations, however.

Women are also obligated to give gifts to the poor on Purim. A married woman may fulfill the mitzvah through her husband. Ideally, however, the husband should inform his wife that he has given matanos la'evyonim for her, as well.

Children who are dependent upon their parents' table should still give matanos la'evyonim on their own (Aruch HaShulchan 694:2).

Rav Moshe Feinstein, zt"l, ruled that one may fulfill the mitzvah of matanos la'evyonim with a check. This is true even if the check is post-dated.

One may fulfill the mitzvah of matanos la'evyonim by giving the money even to a young child who is considered poor.

Matanos la'evyonim may be given anonymously. This is the ideal form of fulfilling the mitzvah.

There is a debate as to whether it is preferable to give many poor people a minimum amount of matanos la'evyonim or to give just a few people a significant amount of matanos la'evyonim. The Bach (siman 695) writes that it is preferable to give more people the lesser amount. Rav Elyashiv, zt"l, is quoted (Shvus Yitzchak 8:2 as cited in Kovetz Halachos, p. 92) that it is preferable to give fewer people a more significant amount. Since either way one fulfills the mitzvah, one should perform it in the manner in which one feels most inspired toward dveikus Bashem.

When does Purim Shtick end and Chillul Hashem begin?

Students like pulling shtick in schools during the month of Adar. Allowing four or five chickens to run around in school is extraordinarily funny. But what about the follow up? What happens afterward? What is the end plan? Is it up to the custodian to figure out what to do with chicken after the Purim prank? Is this not an extraordinary Chillul Hashem if there is no endgame plan?

Or what about an SUV pulling a wooden platform with a table, chairs, food and a mock Purim Seudah with five Chassidim singing "Ad delo yadah?" It is very funny, but is it also a Chillul Hashem?

Or how about appearing in costumes that the public might find to be racist in nature? Is that also not considered a Chillul Hashem?

Some people think that an out and out safety violation, done with no permit and clearly illegal, and one that blocks traffic – even temporarily is a Chillul Hashem.

Others would argue that when there is humor involved – there is no Chillul Hashem. But that is not necessarily the case. If a certain percentage of people are not amused and consider it dangerous and foolish – that too would constitute a Chillul Hashem.

WHO IS COMMANDED IN IT

Every Jew is commanded not to desecrate Hashem's Name, as the pasuk states: "Lo sechalalu es shaim kodshi." The Mitzvah is listed in the 613 Mitzvos of the Rishonim and in the Sefer haChinuch 295. Indeed, if someone causes others to make Chillul Hashems – the Shulchan Aruch rules that he should be put in Cherem (YD 334).

Clearly, even if it is on or near Purim, we should carefully weigh whatever we do to ensure that no Chillul Hashem come about because of our action.

WHAT CONSTITUTES CHILLUL HASHEM

The Rambam (Yesodei Torah 5:4) explains that Chillul Hashem is actually the opposite of Kiddush Hashem. This is a good rule of thumb to follow when one wishes to explore what exactly is a Chillul Hashem. Nonetheless, it is also important to examine what Chazal tell us specifically. The lack of clarity on the issue has created a situation where it could reasonably be said that one man's Kiddush Hashem is another man's Chillul Hashem.

For example, some people think that show of strength is an example of Kiddush Hashem. Others feel that an abuse of strength is, in actuality, a grave Chillul Hashem. It is thus important to see what Chazal and Poskim tell us in order to have a better gauge of the issue. It is not that this examination will resolve any issues between people who are arguing points among each other. But, hopefully, it will give a number of us greater insights.

THE DIFFERENT CATEGORIES

Chillul Hashem can be categorized in different ways.

1] There are a number of different categories of Chillul Hashem that are differentiated in some of the Rishonim.

2] There are Aveiros that the Psukim in the Torah call a Chillul Hashem.

3] There are behaviors that, no matter who the Jew actually is, also constitute a Chillul Hashem.

We will begin with the three different categories found in the Rishonim.

One category is when one if forced to violate one of the three cardinal sins that we must give up our lives for. If someone did not do so, this is a Chillul Hashem according to Sefer HaMitzvos (#63).

A second category is whenever one purposefully does an Aveirah out of spite – this too is considered a Chillul Hashem (Sefer HaMitzvos, ibid).

THE IMPORTANT PERSON CATEGORY

A third category is when an important person does something that causes people to talk – even if it would generally not be considered an Aveirah (Shabbos 51b). This is considered a Chillul Hashem because people will learn from him. The Gemorah explains that greater the person is the more careful he must be.

According to the SMAG #2 and SMaK #85, however, category three is even if is not an important person but a regular Talmid Chochom whose actions cause people to talk – this too is Chillul Hashem. These authorities also say that when a Jew does any action that will cause Goyim to say, "The Jews have no Torah" – this is a Chillul Hashem.

DEBATE AS TO REASON FOR THE "IMPORTANT PERSON" CATEGORY

There is actually a debate as to the reason for the third category of a great person. Is it because he has a higher standard in which to comply with? This is what Rabbeinu Yonah (Avos Mishna 4:4) and the Rambam (Maamar Kiddush Hashem) write. Others understand it because other people will learn from him. Other Rishonim hold that it is because the Torah will be lessened in the eyes of others because of him (Rashi on tractate Shabbos 33a).

EXAMPLES OF CATEGORY THREE

What are examples of category three? The Gemorah (Yuma 86a) gives us illustrations. Rav gives an example of a Talmid Chacham that doesn't pay the butcher bill right away. Rav Yochanan gives as an example of Chillul Hashem of a Talmid Chochom that goes without Torah and without Tefillin for 4 amos. Rav Yochanan's explanation assumed that the onlooker does not realize that the Talmid Chochom just had a marathon session of Torah study and did not have the strength to continue further or the strength of intent to wear the Tefillin properly.

There are some observations that can be made from these illustrations. In regard to Chillul Hashem, according to Rabbi Yochanan, "perception is reality." According to Rav, we have established the notion that it also involves a Middah, a character trait, or behavior and not just an actual sin.

WHAT THE TORAH CALLS CHILLUL HASHEM

There are specific Aveiros that the Torah itself specifically calls Chillul Hashem (See, for example, VaYikra 19:12). Most of these have to do with falsely swearing (shavuos) (See Rashi Taanis 23a), although giving one's child to the Molech (VaYikra 18:21) is also called a Chillul Hashem by the Torah.

Abusing justice by the judges is also a grave Chillul Hashem.

The Gemorah will also provide Psukim that back up the idea that certain activities such as going to Goyish courts is a grave Chillul Hashem (Gittin 88b).

Anything having to with Avodah Zarah (See Rabbeinu Yona Avos 4:4 based on Yechezkel 20:39) is also considered a Chillul Hashem.

GENERAL CHILLUL HASHEMS CAUSED BY PEOPLE

Anyone who sins and causes others to sin – choteh umachti es harabbim is actively being mechalel shaim Hashem (Rashi Yuma 86a).

Another form of Chillul Hashem is when it is pointed out to the world that Klal Yisroel is not doing their job. The Beis Yoseph explains (YD 254) that if a poor person needs to be supported through gentiles – this is a situation of Chillul Hashem. It is, in fact, forbidden for him to do so unless he has nothing to eat. Regardless, it is forbidden for us, the community, to allow the situation to continue.

If Jews are aware that someone Jewish is going to falsely swear in front of gentiles that he does not owe money, when the gentile knows that he does – this is a situation of Chillul Hashem. The Jews must stop him from swearing falsely and rather must work it out with the gentile. This is a ruling in the Ramah in Shulchan Aruch in the laws of Shvuos (YD 239:1).

Generally speaking, we are permitted to take donations from a gentile for a synagogue. However, if the gentile gave it to something specific in shul – we may not change it for anything else because of the Chillul Hashem aspect of it. One may do so, however, under certain circumstances if the donation was made by a Jew. [TaZ's explanation of ruling in Shulchan Aruch YD 259:6]

The Bach in a responsa (#111, old) cites the Sefer Chassidim (#829) that if it is the custom among the gentiles to forbid a certain food because a horrible sin was done with it– then Jews should also refrain from eating it. This is on account of Chillul Hashem.

Publicizing a previously performed Aveirah that was unknown may also be a form of Chillul Hashem (see Tehillim 32:1 from Yuma 86a.) Therefore, when an Aveirah is not known publically one should not say a public vidui.

Physical relations with gentiles is also considered a Chillul Hashem (Rambam Issurei Biah 12:6).

Whenever it is possible to minimize a Chillul Hashem we should do this. This is seen from many Poskim, for example, Chsam Sofer (OC Vol. I #61). One such illustration, an extreme one, can be seen from the following idea:

Even though we no longer have the ability to deal with cases of capital punishments – there are times when Bais Din must act out of Migdar Milsa, especially out of Chillul Hashem. There was such a case where a person [warning: impending euphemisim] "blessed" Hashem and he was punished most severely because of the Chillul Hashem involved (See Teshuvos HaRosh 17:8 cited in Darchei Moshe CM 425).

What is shocking about this latter illustration is that nowadays we cannot perform capital punishment and if we do, it would constitute a capital offense on us as well. And yet to prevent Chillul Hashem, Beis Din allowed it in that instance, in order to minimize the Chillul Hashem of someone "blessing" Hashem. It is this author's belief that the very term for the prohibition is referred to by the sages as "Blessing Hashem" in order to minimize the Chillul Hashem of the entire idea. [It should be noted that nowadays this ruling of the Rosh is not applicable at all.]

HOW HASHEM DEALS WITH CHILLUL HASHEM

The Gemorah tells us (Kiddushin 40a) Ain Makifin b'Chillul Hashem – this means that Hashem pays back (in punishment) a Chillul Hashem right away. What this means is subject to some interpretation (two views even being found in the Gemorah), but we see from all of this the gravity of Chillul Hashem.

CONCLUSION

It would seem that if even a significant minority of the public would perceive it as a Chillul Hashem – then it is – even if we personally do not think so. But regardless of our perception, it is clear that every activity or endeavor that is in the public eye should be carefully weighed to ensure that we do not violate this most fundamental principle. This should be done by asking responsible Rabbonim whose sense of achrayus to the Torah community is unimpeachable.

The Origin of Purim Costumes

One family dressed up as Tzedakah boxes. Another person dressed up as a Shabbos table. One Brooklyn family is dressing up as a team of basketball players. The person in the picture is dressed up like an animal, and davening in shul.

Regardless of the costume, dressing up is definitely NOT one of our run-of-the-mill Minhagim.

Generally, our Minhagim deal with simanim – signs that indicate good mazel rather than bad fortune.They deal with eating or not eating specific foods- Example: Shavuos we eat milchigs, Chanukah – latkes, Rosh HaShana – honey.We don't eat nuts or chrein during Yomim Noraim. Our other Minhagim deal with special Tefilos at special places:Kaparos with chicken or money, Tashlich by the water.

But dressing up? Where and when did this come from?

FIRST MENTION

The first mention of the notion of Jews dressing up in costume seems to be in the responsa of one of our Poskim from Italy, Rav Yehudah Mintz (Responsa #17). Rav Mintz lived in the late 1400's and was niftar in Venice in 1508.The Teshuvah says that there is no prohibition involved in dressing up on Purim even in dressing like a woman – since the reason is for Simchah and not for the purpose of immorality – to violate Torah law.

The Ramah quotes the Psak in Shulchan Aruch Orech Chaim (696:8).

STEINSCHNEIDER'S DILEMNA

Moritz Steinschneider, (1816-1907) the great bibliographer whose impact and opinions are still felt today, brilliant though he was, cannot fathom that the minhag developed independently.He attributes the development of the Minhag to the direct influence of the Roman Carnival. Carnival is a festive season which occurs immediately before the Catholic season of Lent. The Roman Carnival involved a public celebration and or parade that combined elements of a circus, the wearing of masks and public street partying. People would dress up in masquerade during these celebrations.Carnival is a festival traditionally held in Roman Catholic and, to a lesser extent, Eastern Orthodox societies. It originated in Italy and was held in February.

But our Minhag did not come from Roman Carnival.It is not that we believe that cultural diffusion does not exist. We do.

But its application must be tempered with rational precision and reason.We must always display a cautious intellectual approach.Scholars who know what Klal Yisroel is actually all about, know that this particular type of cultural diffusion is about as likely as eggnog consumption and Chrismas Caroling affecting the behavior of Yeshiva boys on a Purim.

CANNOT HAVE COME FROM THE ROMAN CARNIVAL

It simply would not have happened. End of story. The apperception of the Roman Carnival in Torah circles was beyond the pale of acceptable activity even to mimic. This cannot be the source – especially so close to the time of Rav Yehudah Mintz, who sanctioned its use.

No, we must look for other sources in order to find truth. Steinschneider's theory is just too pat. We must also bear in mind that silence in the Seforim and responsa literature does not necessarily indicate absence in normative Jewish practice. A Minhag could exist and yet not be mentioned in the Seforim or Teshuvos until much later.

The Apter Rebbe, Rav Avrohom Yehoshua Heschel, was known as the Ohaiv Yisroel. He writes (Ohaiv Yisroel Shmos Section on Parshas Zachor) that one of the reasons why we dress up in masquerade on Purim is to show that the miracle of Purim came from something that actually would have initially caused us much grief. This, says the Apter Rebbe, stresses that the greatest joy lies in the knowledge that the opposite result might very well have happened. A good theory, but one that, perhaps, may sound more likely to be a post-development rationalization than the original cause of the Minhag.

Rav Yitzchak Weiss zatzal, author of the Siach Yitzchak and student of the Shaivet Sofer, explains (Siman 380) that the origin of the custom to dress up in masks is to highlight the fact that Haman hid his hate for the Jewish people when approaching Achashveirosh for permission to destroy Klal Yisroel. Hashem responded, midah Keneged midah – measure for measure – by sending Eliyahu – disguised as Charvonah. Eliyahu too was hiding his real intent – to defend the Jewish people. Here, the idea of hiding, and a mask as a central theme of Purim seems likely. It may very well have been the idea that spurred on the Minhagin Klal Yisroel to wear masks.

The Bnei Yissaschar (on Adar 9:1) cites a Maharam Chagiz who quotes the Gemorah in Megilah (12a). The Gemorah explains that the Jewish people only did things "Lifnim" – hidden – So Hashem as well only did things "Lifnim" – hidden.

The theme of hiding and its association with Purim, therefore, is found explicitly in the Gemorah itself. Could it have developed just then? Perhaps, but it is hard to imagine that it developed back then and no mention of this custom was made from 500 CE until the late 1400's.

The mystery continues.

THE TOSFOS COMMENT

However, there is a Tosfos in tractate Rosh haShana (3a) that might be very enlightening here. The Tosfos deal with a fascinating episode in Parshas Chukas in the book of BaMidbar (21:1).The Cnaani in the Negev (the south) hear that Klal Yisroel has arrived and go out to do battle with them.Rashi identifies the incongruity.The Negev??Why, that is Amalek!

Rashi's conclusion is that it was Amalekites who spoke in the Cnaani dialect so that Klal Yisroel will pray to Hashem that the Cnaanim be handed over to them and not the Amalekites!

Our Tosfos, however, add more.They write that the Amalekites changed not only their voices and dialect, they changed their clothing too.They cite the person who wrote the piut for Parshas Zachor – Ksus VeLashon Shineh – Clothing and language he (or they) did change!

So here is the theory, then.

It is France and Germany, not Italy.The Paytan for Parshas Zachor has written that they changed their clothing – referring to the Amalekites. Jews see it. Parshas Zachor is close to Purim. Very close.Some regular people read the piut. They may think, perhaps, that it refers to Jews..The scholars among them realize that it refers to Amalekites, but Haman is from Amalek anyway.

On Purim we are Marbeh BeSimcha. It is in the Piut. They begin to dress up, like Haman.

The Minhag catches on.The Talmidei Chachomim of Germany accept it.

THE PRACTICE TRAVELS TO ITALY

Soon the practice travels to Italy. Steinschneider cannot resist and attributes it to the Roman Carnival. But he errs. It is much likelier that it came from the Piut for Parshas Zachor.The origin is a kasher minhag b'Yisroel from German-Jewry.

BACK TO THE APTER RAV

And now we go back to the Apter Rav — the Ohaiv Yisroel.He writes that one of the reasons why we dress up in masquerade on Purim is to show that the miracle of Purim came from something that actually would have initially caused us much grief.This, says the Apter Rebbe, stresses that the greatest joy lies in the knowledge that the opposite result might very well have happened.It is a Minhag that brings us ever closer to the true Dveikus Bashem and Simchah that lies at the heart of what Purim is all about.

DRUNK ON THE CONCEPT NOT ON WINE

Let us, with this in mind, remember the words of the Nesivus Shalom regarding drinking on Purim.He writes that the word "wine" is absent in the formulation of the Shulchan Aruch. "Chayav adam libsumei bePuraya ad delo yada."

The reason is clear.We must become inebriated with the concept of Purim and not with wine.The concept of Purim is that Hashem is very close and that we can achieve remarkable Dveikus Bashem at this time.No matter how distant we are — even if we are "Arur Haman" in terms of our general distance from Hashem— we can become, at this particular time of Purim, as close as Boruch Mordechai.

The nation of Israel can achieve a remarkable degree of real genuine Dveikus Bashem. We can do so like no other people can.When we dress up, therefore, let us appreciate the significance and the Taamim brought down by the Apter Rav, the Bnei Yissaschar and the Siach Yitzchak.This Purim, let us discover the talent that lies within us in this area.If we can do this, we can achieve both a personal Geulah as well as one for all of Klal Yisroel Amain.

An Overview of Mishloach Manos

THE MITZVAH

Mordechai and his Beis Din enacted that on the day of Purim each person must send a gift of at least two portions of food to a friend. This is seen from the verse in Megilas Esther, "Umishloach manos ish l'reyehu."

THE REASONS

What is the reason behind the mitzvah of shalach manos? Two reasons are brought down. The Terumas HaDeshen (Siman 111) writes that it is to ensure that the recipients not run out of food items to serve for their meals.

The Manos HaLevi on Megillas Esther (9:19), written by Rav Shlomo Alkabetz and cited by the Chasam Sofer, writes an altogether different reason: to increase peace and brotherly love. This is the opposite of the characterization of the Jewish people by Haman as a nation "Mefuzar umefurad" spread and standing apart on account of internal arguments.

PREAMBLE AND INTENTIONS

The Yesod v'Shoresh HaAvodah writes that one should recite the following preamble before fulfilling the Mitzvah:

לשם יחוד קודשא בריך הוא הריני מוכן ומזומן לקיים מצות עשה של דברי קבלה ומשלוח מנות איש לרעהו

When performing the Mitzvah one should not just perform it perfunctorily, but should focus on the qualities of the recipient and place within his heart a strong love for his fellow man. He should intend to honor him and to strengthen his inner joy with this package of Shalach Manos.

WHO IS OBLIGATED

Men and women are both included in this mitzvah. The halachah is that men send to men, and women send to women. Women are obligated in the mitzvah because, according to the Mishnah Berurah, "they too were involved in the miracle." A child should be instructed to fulfill the Mitzvah just as one instructs a child to fulfill all the other Mitzvos. The child may send to another child, as the other child is considered his or her peer.

Even a poor person is required to fulfill the mitzvah of mishloach manos. The mitzvah of mishloach manos may not be fulfilled with money, clothing, or other non-food or non-drink items. The mitzvah may only be fulfilled with kosher items.

HOW FANCY?

Another little-known halachah about shalach manos is found in an esoteric Biur Halachah (written by the Chofetz Chaim) in Orach Chaim 695. He writes that the Chayei Adam has proved from a passage in the Talmud Yerushalmi that if one sends a Purim package to a wealthy individual, the package must be a respectable one.

Thus, one should not send something below the kavod of the recipient. The poskim have ruled that a lollipop is not considered chashuv for an adult, nor is a bottle of Poland Spring water or seltzer. To fulfill the Mitzvah, the portions must convey sufficient regard for the recipient.

The Biur Halachah writes that the Ritva's comment on his version of the Talmud Bavli agrees with the Chayei Adam. A careful reading of the Ritva, however, reveals that the Ritva and Chayei Adam are not exactly the same. Both of them require an upgraded Purim package on account of wealth; of that there is no question. However, the Ritva's requirement is of the wealth of the giver—not the recipient. In other words, according to the Ritva, if the giver is very wealthy, his package must reflect that as well and he cannot fulfill the mitzvah with a meager package. Since the Biur Halachah does quote both the Chayei Adam and the Ritva, both would seem to be authoritative.

Therefore, one should not send something below the kavod of the giver or the recipient.

NATURE OF THE PACKAGE

The mitzvah must be fulfilled only with foods that are immediately edible or drinkable. The Magen Avraham, Vilna Gaon, and Chayei Adam hold this way. The Pri Chadash is lenient. We rule in accordance with the former view.

An item that requires further cooking or preparation may be added, but two immediately usable foods must be included, too. It is praiseworthy to send portions to as many friends as possible. It is better, however, to give more matanos la'evyonim than to give more mishloach manos to friends.

THE TWO BLESSINGS MYTH

There is no need for the two different food items to have two separate berachos. This is one of the biggest misconceptions in Hilchos Purim. There is an issue, however, of taking one food item and cutting it in half into two slices. The Aruch haShulchan (OC 695:14) writes that just because one cut it in half it should be considered two foods? Perhaps it is this statement of the Aruch HaShulchan that has caused the two blessing myth to exist. If someone sends another two pieces of meat from two different limbs that tastes slightly different this is considered two foods (Mikraie Kodesh Slman 38).

THROUGH A MESSENGER

Ideally, mishloach manos should be sent through a messenger, rather than be delivered personally. Generally speaking, we say, "Mitzvah bo yoser mi'b'shlucho" — it is a bigger mitzvah to do it oneself rather than through a messenger. Regarding the search for chametz before Pesach, it is better to do it oneself. Here, though, it is different. The Chsam Sopher writes in his commentary to the Talmud (Gittin 22b), that the pasuk says, "and the sending of gifts — mishloach manos" which indicates that it should be done through a messenger. A gift sent through a messenger is fancier and nicer. If one did deliver the mishloach manos oneself, the obligation is still fulfilled.

Virtually all the poskim rule that a goy or a child may be a shaliach for mishloach manos. Rabbi Akiva Eiger, zt"l, was unsure of this, however.

SENT TOGETHER

Must the two foods be sent together? Rav Elyashiv zt"l is of the position that they must. May one of the foods be a liquid? Most authorities hold that one of the foods may certainly be a liquid (except for water), and this is the authoritative view. There is a reading of

Rabbeinu Chananel that holds a liquid may not be one of the two food items. This view is apparently not l'halachah.

GIFT CERTIFICATES

Does sending money to buy food or sending a gift certificate at a restaurant work? Some Acharonim hold that it does, but many hold not. The language of the Rambam (Hilchos Megillah, Chapter 2) seems to indicate that it must be real food and not a gift certificate or money.

REFUSAL OF GIFT

What if a package is prepared and the recipient responds with a "No, thank you?" Has the sender fulfilled the mitzvah in such a case? According to the Terumas HaDeshen it would seem not; according to the second opinion he very well might. It is interesting to note that the Rema in O.C. 695 writes that one has fulfilled the mitzvah. The Pri Chadash questions this position and does not understand it. Our aforementioned Chasam Sofer answers the dilemma by suggesting that the Rema holds like the Manos HaLevi. Perhaps one can point out, however, that even according to the Manos HaLevi, the full effect of the shalach manos has not been achieved. Peace and brotherly love is a two-way street, and the giver doesn't necessarily feel so good if his gift is refused. So how can the Rema be understood? It is only if the recipient responds gently, "Don't worry about it; you don't need to actually give it to me." Rav Ovadiah Yoseph, however, holds that Sephardim should not rely on this Rema and send the shalach manos to someone else.

ANONYMITY

Does the recipient have to know who sent it, or does anonymity work? The Ksav Sofer (responsa O.C. #141) relates the issue to the two reasons mentioned above. He recommends that one be stringent and avoid anonymity. Rav Elyashiv zt"l ruled that one does not fulfill the Mitzvah with anonymity.

LOST OR STOLEN

What happens if the shalach manos that you had sent got lost or stolen? The Birchei Yoseph writes that one must send it again.

THROUGH A CHILD

May one fulfill the mitzvah by sending to a child? The verse in the Megillah uses the term "Umishloach manos ish l'rei'eihu—and the sending of portions each man to his peer." The Aruch HaShulchan permits it and considers a child a "peer." Other poskim disagree with the Aruch HaShulchan. It is, therefore, better to send it to an adult.

TO A MOURNER

What about sending shalach manos to a mourner? The Rema states that one should not send during the entire twelve months of mourning. This halachah is true for Ashkenazim. Sephardim, however, can receive shalach manos during mourning. The mourner, however, should send to one person, but should avoid sending items that arouse great joy. One may send to the spouse of a mourner. The Divrei Malkiel (Vol. V) writes that one may send to one's teacher even if he is a mourner because this is considered similar to a payment of an obligation.

THE PACKAGING

Should at least two of the food items be wrapped separately or in two different containers? Some authorities (the Ben Ish Chai) hold that if they are sent together then the container itself may make it as if it is one food. Thus, Raisin Bran would only be considered one food item unless one separated the raisins from the cereal into two plastic baggies. Others (Sheim M'Shimshon, O.C. #31) write that the container does not make it into one food.

TIMING

When should the shalach manos package be given? It must be given in the daytime and not at night. The mitzvah should also be fulfilled, ideally, before one begins the Purim seudah.

SCHOOL AND SHUL PROGRAMS

What about the school and shul? Schools and shuls often send out a flyer and request you to participate in their shalach manos program when they send out a list of who sent to you. While this idea is fantastic in terms of reducing the waste and excess in shalach manos giving, the givers should be aware that one cannot and does not fulfill the actual mitzvah with this form of giving. Many people are unaware of this fact.

The Different Reasons for Parshas Zachor and What to Have in Mind

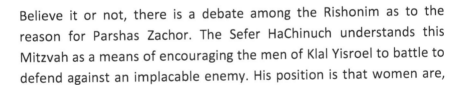

Believe it or not, there is a debate among the Rishonim as to the reason for Parshas Zachor. The Sefer HaChinuch understands this Mitzvah as a means of encouraging the men of Klal Yisroel to battle to defend against an implacable enemy. His position is that women are, in fact, exempt from this Mitzvah.

Not so the Sefer Mitzvos Ketanos (Rav Yitzchok Ben Yosef 1210-1280), also known as the SMaK. He is of the position that the reason is to realize that Hashem saved us from the hand of Amalek and so that we will always be in awe of Him so that we not sin against His will. This position could perhaps be traced to the words of the Targum Yonasan on the verse "Lo Tishkach" (Shmos 25:19). He writes, "v'afilu l'yoma Malka d'meshicha lo tisnashi" – that it applies even to the times of Moshiach.

There is also a fascinating explanation of Yiras Shamayim, fear of Heaven that is provided by the Nesivos Shalom. It is different than the explanation that is commonly given. We are afraid of losing our unique bond and relationship with Hashem – our dveikus to Him. He give a moshol, a parable. Imagine you are drowning in a vast ocean. A lifeguard jumps in and rescues you, You hold on to him for dear life – afraid to let go. You are afraid of losing that connection you have with him.

So too here, Yiras Shamayim, according to this explanation of the Nesivos Shalom is that you are afraid of losing that special relationship that you have with Him.

According to the combined SMaK's and Nesivos Shalom's explanation, we read Parshas Zachor to further cement the notion within us that Hashem saved us from the hand of Amalek and so that we will realize how precious our relationship with Hashem is and that we should be afraid of losing it. This will encourage us not to sin and do aveiros – which will distance ourselves from Him.

According to the Sefer HaChinuch (and also the Ramban's explanation) the obligation is combined with the Mitzvah of destroying Amalek. Many people explain that Amalek represents the epitome of evil. The intent we should have then is that we must fight that which epitomizes evil in all that we can.

Parshas Zachor, the Megillah, and the Barely Bar-Mitzvahed

There are three categories of Jews in Jewish law. There are minors, there are adults and there is a third category which we will term, "The barely bar-Mitzvahed." These three categories, believe it or not, have different halachic statuses. They affect us for Parshas Zachor as well as the Megillah itself.

But let's get some definitions.

The "barely bar-Mitzvahed" is a child who has reached the age of Bar Mitzvah but has not yet demonstrated clear signs of physical maturity.

How is the halacha of the barely Bar Mitzvahed any different from, say, an adult?

NOT FOR BIBLICAL MITZVOS

The general rule of thumb is that we should not rely upon a Barely bar-Mitzvahed to fulfill a full blown biblical Mitzvah for us. Example: A Barely bar-Mitzvahed may recite Kiddush for his mother or sisters on Shabbos morning. He should not do so on Friday night. On Friday night, the obligation to recite the Kiddush is biblical. The words, "Zachor es Yom HaShabbos lekadsho" teach us this according to the Biur Halacha (Orech Chaim 271). On Shabbos morning the obligation is Rabbinic. The Mishna Brurah (on SA OC 271:2) rules that while a Barely bar-Mitzvahed should not be Motzi others for Friday night Kiddush, he may do so for Shabbos morning Kiddush because it is Derabanan.

In hearing Parshas Zachor we fulfill a Torah commandment. May we rely on a barely bar-Mitzvahed to lein it for us? The answer is, "NO."

Shockingly, it could be that we should be relying upon the barely bar-Mitzvahed for the reading of the Megillah either. Why is this so? Rav Yoseph Chaim Sonnenfeld (Responsa Toras Chaim #53) is of the opinion that since Megillah takes the place of Hallel, it is considered to be Biblical on account of a Kal VaChomer! The Turei Even and the Netziv are of the same opinion in terms of treating the obligation to read the Megillah as a biblical obligation.

NOT WELL KNOWN

Interestingly enough, the halachos of the barely bar-Mitzvahed are not so well known. The reason that they are not so well known is because they are generally not taught in school or at home. Perhaps this is because the exact parameters of physical maturity are a topic that people are not so comfortable discussing. As a consequence, knowledge of the Halacha of the barely bar-Mitzvahed has suffered. This is unfortunate because many people inadvertently violate Halacha as a result.

YOM TOV KIDDUSH AND HAVDALLAH

What about Yom Tov Kiddush at night? Since some Poskim rule that this too is Biblical in origin it is perhaps best to be stringent. Certainly, the Yom Tov daytime Kiddush is only Rabbinic and that would be permitted according to all authorities.

How about Havdalah? Here we have a distinction. If the person hearing his Havdallah has not prayed the evening service and did not include the prayer of Atta Chonantanu in his Shmoneh Esreh then he should not hear it from the Barely bar-Mitzvahed. If the person hearing havdallah did recite a form of Havdallah previously, the Havdallah ceremony is only a Rabbinic obligation and the Barely bar-Mitzvahed may recite it. Women, who generally do not daven Maariv, should therefore recite the formula "HaMavdil Bein Kodesh L'chol" before hearing Havdallah from a Barely bar-Mitzvahed.

GENERAL DAVENING AND LEINING

And what about leading the Davening and Leining? Leining is permitted. Leading the Maariv is also permitted. Shacharis, Mussaf, and Mincha are problematic, however. He may be exempting others in Tefillah, a Biblical commandment according to the Rambam. According to the Ramban it may be biblical as well since he is of the opinion that prayer is biblically mandated when it is an Ais Tzarah, a time of difficulty. Modern Poskim have stated that our times qualify for the Ramban's definition as well.

PESACH

On Pesach, if a Barely bar-Mitzvahed did the search for Chometz it is completely acceptable. Why? Because we recite the formula of Bittul in any case, making the Bedikah a Rabbinic obligation (MB 432:8). It follows from this that if the Bittul is not going to be recited for some reason, the Barely bar-Mitzvahed should not be the one doing the search for Chometz.

What about Matzah-baking? Those who are very involved in this Mitzvah are generally more aware of the halachos of the barely bar-Mitzvahed than others. The halacha concerning a boy who has just barely been Bar Mitzvahed is clear. He should not bake the Matzos Mitzvah according to the Biur Halacha (460:1). He may draw the water and measure the flour, however, according to the Misgeres HaShulchan on the Kitzur Shulchan Aruch (OC 110:15).

ROSH HASHANA

For Hataras Nedarim on Erev Rosh haShana, a Barely bar-Mitzvahed should not be one of the three members of the Beis Din. This is the ruling of Rabbi Akiva Eiger in his responsa (Volume I #73). In this author's opinion, this is one of the most common violations of Barely bar-Mitzvahed Halacha.

On Rosh HaShana itself, a Barely bar-Mitzvahed should not blow shofar for others in order for them to fulfill their Mitzvah. If they have already heard the first 30 blasts which are biblical and he is merely fulfilling the one hundred blast quota it would be permitted. The Mateh Efraim 589:7 rules that a Barely bar-Mitzvahed should not even blow Shofar for others on the second day of Rosh HaShana. Presumably, the reason is that we treat the second day of Rosh haShanas as stringently as we do the first day.

SUKKOS

Before Sukkos a person should not purchase his Lulav and Esrog from a Barely bar-Mitzvahed out of concern that the sale of a child may only be effective by Rabbinic law. [This can be easily understood from the fact that in secular law, property cannot be bought and sold by a minor]. The Ksav Sofer (OC 128) rules that we should be stringent regarding this matter. As far as putting up the Schach on a Sukkah, although a child should ideally not do so, a Barely bar-Mitzvahed can according to the Pri Magadim (Siman 14).

A married man whose wife has not yet fulfilled the Mitzvah of Lulav and Esrog (and plans to do so with her husband's set) should not lend his Lulav and Esrog to a Barely bar-Mitzvahed in Shul on the first day of Yom Tov. This is out of concern that, while he is legally capable of accepting the gift, he may not be able to give it back. Rather, he should tell the Barely bar-Mitzvahed to come to his home that afternoon.

What about Tevilas Keilim, immersing our vessels into a Mikvah before we use them to eat? The Pri Magadim (OC 451) rules that regarding glass vessels and other vessels whose obligation of immersion are only Rabbinic we may rely on The barely bar-Mitzvahed to immerse. Therefore, one may not rely upon a Barely bar-Mitzvahed to immerse metal vessels other than ones made of aluminum.

For all of these halachos should the barely bar-Mitzvahed be Motzi others who are barely bar-Mitzvahed? The answer is clearly not. There is a chance that the other Barely bar-Mitzvahed is actually an adult while the person making the Bracha may not be. Therefore, a Barely bar-Mitzvahed should not even fulfill the Mitzvah for other barely bar-Mitzvahed.

WHEN DOES IT END?

When does the status of Barely bar-Mitzvahood end? Is there an age where we can automatically assume, even without evidence, that the young man has passed into full-fledged adulthood? The Mogen Avrohom (beginning of OC 39) writes that when the young man has reached eighteen years of age we can assume that he has reached full-fledged adulthood. Rabbi Akiva Eiger (Responsa OC #7), however, raises the question as to what the Mogen Avrohom's source for this is, as does the Eliyahu Rabbah. The Hagaos Chsam Sofer posits that an error has crept into the text of the Mogen Avrohom and suggests that the Mogen Avrohom really meant to write that it ends at the age of twenty.

DON'T EMBARRASS THEM

It is important to keep in mind that pointing out to a Barely bar-Mitzvahed that he is, in fact, a Barely bar-Mitzvahed may be insulting to him and could possibly hurt his feelings. This could be a negation of the Torah Mitzvah of "VeAhavta L'Rayacha Kamocha," Heaven forbid. Upon further reflection, this could possibly be why, in fact, knowledge of these halachos has not been so widespread. Perhaps the Rabbis who run our educational institutions are aware of the inherent dangers involved here and did not want people to inadvertently insult or hurt people. This is important to keep in mind when observing these halachos.

WHEN TO TEACH IT

The conclusion is that when we do try to observe these halachos we should do so quietly and without fanfare. At what point should the child be taught the halachos of Barely bar-Mitzvahed before his Bar Mitzvah? It would seem that if we do a number of months prior to his Bar Mitzvah this would address the issue of possible embarrassment.

The Purim Seudah

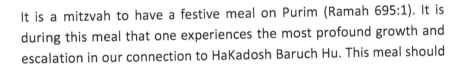

It is a mitzvah to have a festive meal on Purim (Ramah 695:1). It is during this meal that one experiences the most profound growth and escalation in our connection to HaKadosh Baruch Hu. This meal should include meat and wine.

One should also wash on bread at this festive meal because there are many authorities who hold that it is an obligation (Raavya Vol. II Siman 563).

By the same token, it is preferable to have beef during this meal and not just chicken, as there are some authorities who hold that chicken does not fulfill the requirement of simcha.

STATE OF HAPPINESS

A person should eat and drink their seudah in a state of happiness. One should gladden every family member at this meal (See Eliyahu Rabba 695:4 and Rashi Megillah 9:28)

AT LEAST TWO ITEMS

The meal should have at least two items, meat and some other dish (See Rambam 2:15 who learns that the obligation of Mishloach Manos stems from the obligation of the Seudah).

This is at a minimum. Indeed, the Rambam indicates that one should arrange and organize the best meal that one can (Megillah 2:15).

DURING THE DAY

This meal is held during the day. If one holds it at night, he has failed to fulfill his obligation. Nevertheless, one's evening meal should be more festive than usual. One should wear clothing befitting a festival, and rejoice.

OTHER MINHAGIM

There is also a custom to eat a kreplach at the Seudah, which is meat covered with a dough. This is because the entire holiday came about through hidden means (Likutei Maharich).

Some have the custom to eat Hamatsashen at the meal (Taamei HaMinhagim, Aruch HaShulchan and perhaps the Kitzur Shulchan Aruch).

Traditionally, hamantaschen have been made out of poppy seeds, although, of late, there are all sorts of other fillers that have popped up. Why poppy seeds? The minhag was based upon a Ramah in Shulchan Aruch, where he cites the Kol Bo and writes (OC 695:2), "Some say that it is a custom to eat zironim – seeds on Purim, as a commemoration of the seeds that Daniel and his friends ate in Babylonia."

Both the Pri Chadash and the Aruch haShulchan (OC 695:9) pose the following question:

Daniel? This is Purim – about Esther, not Daniel! Also, the Gemorah (Megillah 13a) tells us that Esther also ate seeds when she first came to the palace – Haigai fed it to her. Why then does the Ramah only quote Daniel?

Also, the Mishna Brurah mentions the Gemorah too, but does not address the question of the Pri Chadash and the Aruch haShulchan.

This author would like to propose the following answer.

Esther knew that there was rhyme and reason to her being taken into the palace. She knew that she was in need of a miracle. And now, those in charge of the women who were brought to the palace were offering them anything. She could have had her choice of any kosher food. Why then did she pick seeds?

Esther most certainly was aware of the miracle that happened to Daniel and his friends in the very beginning of Sefer Daniel. After ten days they were healthier and finer than all the others solely on a diet of seeds. This was the beginning of the help that Daniel rendered to his people. Perhaps she should take the same avenue.

With this answer we have greater insight into the minhag of eating poppy seed hamantaschen. Just as there was a miracle that occurred to Klal Yisroel regarding the seeds that Daniel and his friends ate, wherein they adhered strictly to the Kosher dietary laws through seeds and just like Esther tried to follow in those footsteps, so too should we merit miracles by virtue of our adhering carefully to the Torah's dietary laws as symbolized by the poppy seeds.

There is another message about Purim that everyone could gain from. Daniel merited a miracle by keeping kosher. Esther did too. This is the reason behind our custom of eating poppy hamantaschen.

The main Purim meal is held Purim afternoon and is preceded by Minchah. The meal is extended into the night. Most of the meal, however, should be during the day.

Drinks for Yeshiva Boys Who Are Collecting

They come to the door collecting for their Yeshivos. Should one offer them a drink? Yes. But nothing alcoholic – Snapple does the trick as well.

Let us, with this in mind, remember the words of the Nesivus Shalom regarding drinking on Purim. He writes that the word "wine" is absent in the formulation of the Shulchan Aruch. "Chayav adam libsumei bePuraya ad delo yada."

The reason is clear. We must become inebriated with the concept of Purim and not with wine. The concept of Purim is that Hashem is very close and that we can achieve remarkable Dveikus Bashem at this time.No matter how distant we are – even if we are "Arur Haman" in terms of our general distance from Hashem– we can become, at this particular time of Purim, as close as Boruch Mordechai.

Aside from this, the Mitzvah of drinking is only at the Seudah. And there are numerous interpretations which seem more in line with what the guidelines that the Torah requires of us.

One pshat is that ad de lo yada – means ad velo ad bichlal – never get to that point. Rav Avigdor Miller zt"l held that way. The Aruch haShulchan (695:3) states that it means to reach a point where one would be unable to recite an ancient poem with the stanzas "cursed is Haman" and "blessed is Mordechai."

The Remah writes that one is merely required to drink "a little more than usual" on Purim which would cause one to fall asleep.

Another explanation (See Mogain Avrohom 695:3) is that one should drink to the point where one is unable to calculate the gematrias of "cursed is Haman" and "blessed is Mordechai."

The baal haMaor writes that the reason that the Gemorah tells us the story of Rabba killing Rabbi Zeira was to show us why we should not be drinking on Purim.

There is a fascinating Gemorah that backs up this idea. The Talmud Yerushalmi (Tractate Shabbos 8:1) explains that Rabbi Yehudah Bar Illai would only drink wine from Pesach to Pesach. The implication is that Rabbi Yehudah Bar Illai did not drink wine on Purim. The Talmud Bavli has a similar statement in Nedarim (49b).

There are three possible understandings of this passage of the Yerushalmi. The first is that indeed, this is the case, but the halacha is not in accordance with Rabbi Yehudah Bar Illai. The second possibility is that we are misreading the import and implication of this Yerushalmi. The third possibility is that Rabbi Yehudah Bar Illai had a perfectly valid reason not to consume wine on Purim and was in complete accordance with our statement in the Gemorah which is cited by the Shulchan Aruch.

The Shaarei Teshuva (695:2) writes clearly that we should interpret the Yerushalmi in this third method. This third understanding of the Yerushalmi understands that Rabbi Yehuda Ben Illai had a weaker constitution and that drinking wine would actually damage his health, body or general welfare.

WE ARE ALL LIKE RABBI YEHUDAH BAR ILLAI

A very good argument can be made that in contemporary times we all share the status of Rabbi Yehudah Bar Illai.

How so?

According to the National Institute of Health, a very reliable website, [See http://www.niaaa.nih.gov/alcohol-health/alcohols-effects-body], drinking too much – even on a single occasion, can take a serious toll on your health. Here's how alcohol can affect your body:

Brain:

Alcohol interferes with the brain's communication pathways, and can affect the way the brain looks and works. This is even on a single occasion.

Heart:

Drinking a lot, even on a single occasion, can damage the heart, causing problems including:

Cardiomyopathy – Stretching and drooping of heart muscle

Arrhythmias – Irregular heart beat

Stroke

High blood pressure

Liver:

Heavy drinking, over time, can lead to a variety of problems and liver inflammations including:

Steatosis, or fatty liver

Alcoholic hepatitis (single occasion)

Fibrosis

Cirrhosis

Pancreas:

Alcohol causes the pancreas to produce toxic substances that can eventually lead to pancreatitis, a dangerous inflammation and swelling of the blood vessels in the pancreas that prevents proper digestion.

Cancer:

Drinking too much alcohol can, over time, increase the risk of developing certain cancers, including cancers of the:

Mouth

Esophagus

Throat

Liver

Immune System:

Drinking too much can weaken the immune system, making it a much easier target for disease. Drinking a lot on a single occasion slows your body's ability to ward off infections – even up to 24 hours after getting drunk.

According to "Alcohol Use and Abuse," a Harvard Health Publication, the use of alcohol nowadays is fraught with danger, and is often quite damaging to the body. Among the effects are:

Alcohol has some very harmful and permanent effects on developing brains and bodies.

For adolescents ages 15 to 20, alcohol is implicated in more than a third of driver fatalities resulting from automobile accidents and about two-fifths of drowning, r"l.

Drinking interferes with good judgment, leading young people into risky behavior and making them vulnerable to all sorts of other problems.

Teenagers who use alcohol and tobacco are at greater risk of using other drugs.

Teenagers who drink are more likely to develop behavioral problems, including stealing, fighting, and skipping school.

Underage drinking is illegal, and there are and have been some serious consequences and repercussions of arrests.

OTHERS CERTAINLY ARE IN THE RAV YEHUDAH BAR ILLAI STATUS

Let us not make the tragic error that we are above any of these problems. They exist in our communities and often under our very noses. Even if it was not true that alcohol consumption constitutes a "Rabbi Yehudah Bar Illai risk" to a particular individual, the very fact that new and more dangerous technologies have developed in the past century that can greatly increase dangers to other around us, the status of Rabbi Yehudah Ben Illai would apply to others around us. Automobiles did not exist in previous times and cars plus alcohol endanger the welfare of others. In our communities, not one year has gone by in recent years where alcohol consumption did not cause a major tragedy or accident.

As far as the Mitzvah itself is concerned, the opinion of the Ravya (564) and the Mordechai (Megillah Chapter 2) and the response of the Maharil (#56) is that even back in the time of Chazal it was not obligatory, rather it is a "Mitzvah b'almah" – an ideal that is no way obligatory. The Ramah cites these views as halacha.

Some will invariably make the argument that drinking large amounts of alcohol was always the practice. How can we now, all of a sudden, assume that it is a health risk and declare that we all share the status of Rabbi Yehudah Bar Illai?

The answer to this question rests within an answer to yet another question. According to the National Vital Statistic Reports of 2004 (52 #14), the life span of Americans has nearly doubled since 1900. What modern innovation contributed the most to the increase in human longevity? The answer is most likely, the refrigerator and the decline in the use of salt as a preservative. Salt kills. We have lowered our consumption of it and now we live longer. The same is true with alcohol.

It has been said that the Shaarei Teshuvah's understanding of the Yerushalmi is the one that is halachically most cogent as it does not posit a contradiction of sources. It is also clear that many people fall within the rubric of the exemption of Rabbi Yehudah Bar Illai, and should not drink to the point of anywhere near drunkenness – even according to the Poskim that do not agree with the Ramah's reading.

So the next time singing Yeshiva boys come to the door for Tzedaka for their Yeshiva, reach for the checkbook and the Snapple.

Bris Milah and Rosh Chodesh – A New Innovation

Rosh Chodesh is a special and festive occasion that symbolizes the renewal of the Jewish people. The Mishna Brurah writes (419:2) that when Rosh Chodesh falls on Shabbos it is a Mitzvah to add a special dish on account of Rosh Chodesh. It would seem that the same logic would apply to a Bris Milah that falls out on Rosh Chodesh – that one should add an extra dish or course that would not normally be served at the meal of a Bris.

The Tur (Siman 419) cites a Psikta that states in regard to Rosh Chodesh that if one adds to Rosh Chodesh [in a seudah] then that person receives additions from Heaven. Ostensibly, this would be no different in the meal held in honor of a Bris Milah.

The Bach writes that on a two day Rosh Chodesh that occurs on Shabbos and Sunday, it would not be sufficient to merely add to the Shabbos meal since it would not be identifiable that it is being done for Rosh Chodesh. The Yaavetz writes that one should just have a larger Melaveh Malka than one is accustomed to have.

Rav Ovadiah Yosef zt"l has a different approach. In Responsa Chazon Ovadiah Vol. I #8, he writes that one can fulfill two mitzvos with the same kezayis. However, the Mishna Brurah clearly indicates that there should be a recognizable difference – unlike Rav Ovadiah Yoseph's view.

THE QUESTION

The question is what food can be added that would not normally be found at a Bris? In other words, merely adding another dish would not be effective because no one would know that this dish was added specifically for Rosh Chodesh!

Possible answers were suggested by Mark Gross of Sharmel Caterers, "For a milchig Bris, you can have a cheese noodle kugel. This is not a dish that is served at a Bris in general, yet it would fulfill your requirement of something extra for Rosh Chodesh." For those that have fleishigs at their Bris Milah seudah he provided another suggestion. "For fleishigs you can serve kishka. This is not something that is served at fleishig brises either, and you can tell that it was added on for some other purpose."

The Two Types of Bris Milah

Many people describe two types of Bris Milahs. They describe the kind with waiters, hot dishes, crepes and fancy chafing dishes. At those affairs, they offer scrambled eggs, hot pancakes with syrup, white fish and all sorts of fish platters, including the much liked sable. The other Bris is more simple – the kind that has tuna and egg salad, assorted rolls and danishes. Both types, of course, have fresh bagels, orange juice, and coffee.

This article is about two different types of Bris Milahs, but not the culinary type.

This article discusses halachic and procedural differences in the manner in which the Bris Milah is performed. The two types are different not only in the manner and style of how the Bris is actually performed – they also produce different physical results as well.

The best way to characterize the two different methods are with the following terms:

- The two-step method

- The one-step method

There are mohelim that practice the two-step method. This is the more traditional method – practiced for thousands of years. This method is near universal among Chassidish Mohalim. There are mohelim that practice the one-step method. In America, in the Litvish world, this is the most common method.

Few mohalim, however, will practice both methods, but some do.

Mohalim are also rather territorial about their particular method. It is a somewhat touchy issue with many of them, so proceed with caution when and if you bring up the subject.

What follows is not for the faint of heart – so proceed with caution. However, the material under discussion is Torah – and we are obligated in learning all sections of Torah – even those that can make us a little queasy. So here goes.

THE ORLAH HAS TWO PARTS

The Orlah actually has two parts – the outer part and the inner part. The inner part is referred to as the "or hapriyah." The inner part is actually termed a "mucous membrane" and is similar to the inside of an eyelid. Imagine the lip – the outer side is dryer skin, while the inner side is not.

THE TWO STEP METHOD

In the two step method, the upper part is lifted upward and cut with the Mohel's knife. This is the first step. The inner part is peeled back and torn with the Mohel's sharpened thumbnail, and then pulled down toward the body of the baby. This is the second step. The lowered inner part eventually fuses together with the remnant of the upper part.

The thumbnail's role in the second step is even mentioned in the Midrash. The Yalkut Shimoni (#723) on the verse in Tehillim, "Kol Atzmosai Tomarnah" – states as follows: Dovid HaMelech says, "I praise You (Hashem) with each of my limbs and fulfill Mitzvos with them.. fingernails – to perform Priyah with them.."

THE ONE STEP METHOD

In the one-step method, the Mohel uses a probe to pry loose the upper and lower Orlah from the rest of the body. He will then often use a hemostat to grasp both the inner orlah along with the upper orlah. A hemostat looks like a scissors, but it is actually a clamp type of device. Generally speaking, the inner Orlah does not go up with the outer Orlah so easily without the hemostat. When they are clamped together – it does go up. The mohel then takes his Mohel knife and cuts both off together. In this method, the Milah and the Priyah are accomplished at the same time. There are one step Mohalim who are able to grab it in a manner that they can cut the inner orlah as well – even without a hemostat.

The physical differences between the one-step method and the two-step method are not minimal. The one step method actually takes off more of the inner skin. The two-step method involves tearing, peeling, and moving the inner part of the Orlah downward, but not actually removing it.

Rabbi Moshe Bunim Perutinsky z"l, author of the Sefer HaBris, writes that although in the time of the Rishonim, the one step method was not used, it was used in the times of the Gaonim. He admits that the one step method was not commonly done in Europe nor in the time of the Rishonim or Acharonim.

THE BENEFITS OF THE ONE STEP METHOD

Rabbi Perutinsky claims (See Sefer HaBris p. 206) that there are five benefits to the one step method:

- There is less blood.

- The operation is much faster.

- The wound heals quicker.

- There are no problems of the Or HaPriyah ever coming back to necessitate a possible Rabbinic re-do.

- When a hemostat is used there is no concern that too much or too little of the Orlah will be cut.

He also writes that these benefits make the one step method preferable to the two-step method. It is just that not everyone was able to do it in this manner and that the two step method was easier, and therefore, more common.

THE WORDING OF THE SHULCHAN ARUCH

The proponents of the two step method claim that the wording of both the Rambam (Hilchos Milah chapter 2) and the Shulchan Aruch (YD 264:3) is clearly like them. It states that first one does the Milah and then one does the Priyah. Indeed, the language of the Rosh is that the blessing of "lehachniso lebriso shel avrohom avinu" is recited in between the Milah and the Priyah.

Dayan Weiss (Minchas Yitzchok Vol. IX #100) cites a number of Acharonim that condemn any changes in the traditional method of Milah. He writes that Heaven forbid for someone to change the method of the way Bris Milah has been performed throughout the ages and strongly urges that the Milah be done with the two step method.

Rav Perutinsky responds that this is not considered a change since Rav Hai Gaon used to do it in this manner. He also writes that had the Acharonim seen the responsum of Rav Hai Gaon they would never have written against the one step method.

Rav Vosner zt"l, the author of the Shaivet HaLevi (Vol. IV #133) writes that since the Rambam and Shulchan Aruch essentially ignored the responsum, they either disagreed with it or felt that the responsum was of dubious authenticity. The Rivash in Responsa #165 also dismisses a different responsum attributed to Rav Hai Gaon.

In contrast to Dayan Weiss zt"l and Rav Vosner zt"l, Rav Moshe Feinstein zt"l (Igros Moshe YD I #155) does not consider the one-step method a problem at all, but states that "meheyos tov" to leave over some of the or haPriyah to be removed by the fingernail – since this method is explicitly mentioned in the Midrash. Nonetheless, it is this author's recollection that Rav Yisroel Belsky zt"l, a talmid muvhak of Rav Moshe Feinstein, still did the two step method.

The Sefer Milah K'hilchasa recommends that if one does the one-step method that one should actually leave over ½ of the or hapriyah in order to fulfill the opinion of the Yad Ketanah in the Shulchan Aruch as to what would define priyah.

Both methods hold that the other method is valid. The question is which one is preferable. One should, of course, consult with one's own Rav or Posaik as to which method to pursue in this regard.

Pesach Wine and Yayin Nesach: The Whys

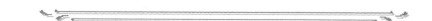

Choosing the Pesach wine is a pastime employed by many people this time of the year. One main question people have is whether to buy mevushal wine (cooked wine) or to by non-mevushal.

Although the halacha allows for both cooked wines and non-cooked wines for the recitation of Kiddush (See Ramah SA OC 272:8), some people are stringent and try to use wine that is not cooked at all (see Mishna Brura 272:23 and Kitzur Shulchan Aruch 77:6). However, there is a downside to this stringency. The downside is that non-cooked wines are more susceptible to become prohibited under the concept of Stam Yainam.

What is Stam Yainam and why are these wines prohibited? Also, what are the details of these laws? What may be done with wine and what may not be done? In order to better understand the concept, a brief excursion might be instructive.

The Odyssey is an ancient Greek tale by Homer that is studied in high schools across the country. In it appears our instructive line:

"To misuse a stranger in the house of Odysseus is a shame. Now let us pour out a libation of wine to the gods, and then let each man go to his home."

Clearly, it was the norm in ancient times to pour libations of wine to gods and deities that were commonly worshipped. Homer's casual insertion of the line is tantamount to ordering a beer in today's society.

All this, of course, is quite foreign to Judaism and to the Torah way of life. To Judaism, the so-called "gods" and anything offered to them – particularly these libations were an affront to the very purpose of creation. The Torah and the Rabbis, as seen in the laws of Yayin nesach and Stam Yainam, showed a passionate indignation toward these offerings. Why? Why the intensity?

The answer of course lies in the Jewish conception of Hashem. Not only is Hashem the Creator of the world, but He is the source of all that is good. He is also desirous of the ultimate good of mankind – all of mankind – and rewards good and punishes evil.

Idol-worship and all its accouterments form the anti-thesis of Hashem's purpose in the world. Wine libations that are offered to the gods serve to cement man's allegiance to the negation of the Divine purpose and message in the world. And this lies in stark contrast to Torah and the ultimate mission of the Jewish people.

But it is more than this. It is the casualness of it all too. The message and mission of the Divine plan should be all-consuming. The casual disregard for Hashem and for the purposes for His creating us, as is typically manifest in the example of the Odyssey, highlights all that is wrong with what mankind is doing. It is not just evil, but the very banality of evil which gives rise to that passionate indignation of Judaism.

Just as the observance of the Sabbath affirms and attests to the Hand of Hashem in the Creation of the world – the wine libations to "gods" attempt to deny Hashem, His purpose in creation, and His system of reward and punishment. It denies the Divine and prophetic messages of Chessed, love, acts of lovingkindness, universal brotherhood, and Divine service.

On Rosh HaShana we pray for that ultimate time when all the nations in the world will unite under one banner to perform the Divine Will with one united and complete heart. And just as a banner or a flag represents the hopes, ideals, and aspirations of a nation, so too does an "anti-flag." Wine libations to gods are the physical embodiment of this "anti-flag" negating the Divine message and purpose in the world.

Jewish philosophy has always posited that the existence of the One Hashem is intuitive by reason. Any thinking person can see Hashem's existence by reason alone. The lack of this knowledge, the eclipsing of Hashem is brought about only by dint of desire. The gods and the wine gifts to them are a clever ruse of the Yetzer HaRah to deflect mankind from his true role and purpose in the world.

And the Jewish role is precisely the opposite. We see from many passages and psukim in Tanach (e.g. Hashem's concern for Pharoah, Amos 9:7, Sefer Yonah) that, far from being unconcerned with the fate of the gentiles around us, the Jewish role is to be a light unto the nations to ultimately bring the nations of the world back to the belief in ethical monotheism. This reason is also reflected in the idea that wine can lead to the abandonment of our mission in numerous ways including intermarriage.

Our purpose eventually is to cause man to reflect upon his true role and purpose in the world. Our first concern is to make sure that we are up that task, however. That each member of the Jewish nation develops Dveikus Bashem – that close bond with the Hashem – which lies within us. The role of or la'amim is the fulfillment of the true destiny of the Jewish people – one we were Divinely chosen to fulfill as we recite in the Kiddush, "Ki vanu vacharta mikol ha-amim."

The fulfillment of this role involves the development of a focused purpose in what and who we are and what we should be doing. The issue of wine is so severe in the eyes of guardians of the Torah tradition that they even forbade the use of wine if it was handled by anyone who is not fully committed to the message of Torah and Judaism.

These laws are as follows: If a gentile grabbed hold of an open bottle of wine and swirled it, even if he or she did not lift the bottle nor touch the wine – the wine is forbidden. (SA YD 124:17) According to the Ramah, however, because of various mitigating factors – if there is a significant loss involved, one may be lenient – even if the wine bottled was lifted and shaken or stirred.

If the gentile held a closed bottle whether it was either full or partially full, the bottle is permitted. The reason is that this is not the manner of pouring a libation. If the gentile held an open bottle and lifted it but did not swirl the contents around, the wine is still permitted. If the gentle merely touched the open bottle this is certainly permitted.

The prohibition extends even to leaving an unsealed bottle of wine with a gentile.

It is important to bear all this in mind when putting away the wine for the Seder and there is a concern that a gentile will make use or pour the wine. As we have seen from the laws, not all wine that is left out has become unkosher. It is important to reflect upon the message that lies within this prohibition – especially during this holiday where we celebrate the formation of Klal Yisroel as a nation. A Chag Kasher VeSameach!

Pizza Wars, Beis Din, and the

New York Times

This is one of those halachic wars that it made in into the pages of the New York Times herself, and written by a journalist with a decidedly Irish last name – Corey Killgannon.

It involves two very avant-garde pizza shops. There is Basil Pizza and Wine Bar, owned by Daniel Branover – which is highly successful. It has been opened since 2010 and features high end specialty pizzas – the kind with thin-crusts and uniquely blended specialty sauces.

And then there is the new store on the block, Calabria which opened up a month ago – and is in direct competition with Basil.

They too offer think crusts and specialty sauces. Both shops are in Crown Heights and, in fact, Calabria opened across the street from

Basil. The second shop looks quite different from the sleek and modern first shop. There is Hebrew writing on the ceiling. The menu is also chalked on a blackboard.

Even though they looked different, the pizza was pretty similar in appearance.

Basil's took Calabria to the Beis Yoseph Beis Din in Boro Park. The Beis Din ruled that Calabria has to go to regular New York style pizza. They did, sort of. It seems they still may be selling some of the similar pizza as well. The Dayanim of the Beis Yoseph Beis Din actually took an Uber to Crown Heights to see things for themselves. They looked at the menu, the prices and the geographic location.

THE ISSUE – HASAGAS GVUL

The issue under discussion is called in Halacha – Hasagas Gvul. The Gemorah in Bava Basra (21b) writes that one cannot set up a fishing net that is too close to the net of another fisherman – and catch all of his fish. The fish were heading toward the original net.

THE GRINDING MILL CASE

The Gemorah further discusses another case. In the other case someone is operating a grinding mill in an alley. Someone else opens up shop as well. Is this also a problem of hasagas gvul?

THE TWO OPINIONS

The first opinion, (that of Rav Huna), says it is and that the first mill owner can prevent the second from opening up. The second view, Rav Huna Bar Rav Yehoshua, says that it is permitted. The second view states that the second mill owner can say, "Whoever will come to me will come to me and whoever will come to you will come to you." The Gemorah indicates that the second view is the normative view – provided that the new competitor does not look to directly damage the first.

RULING OF THE SHULCHAN ARUCH

The Shulchan Aruch (CM 156:5) follows this second view. The second view is qualified, however. It is only permitted to one who lives in the same area. The Tur indicates, however, that if the outsider pays the local taxes he may open in that area. Rav Yoseph Karo, in his Shulchan Aruch accepts this view. However, the Ramah cites a different caveat – that he may only open in a different alley way in that city (See Tosfos Bava Basra 21b "v'ee.")

THE AVIASAF'S VIEW

There is also a view cited by the Mordechai (Bava Basra Siman 516). This view is that of the Aviasaf who forbids opening up a store in an entrance to a cul de sac alley if there is a further store higher toward the cul de sac.

In his commentary on the Tur, Rav Karo claims that this view follows the rejected first opinion.

The Ramah in his Darchei Moshe (CM 156:4) explains the Aviasaf (also cited in the Hagaos Mordechai) in accordance with the second view.

There is also a fascinating responsum of the Rashba (3:83). He writes that while the second store may open – he cannot actively go after and pursue customers of the first business.

In our case of the two avant garde Pizza shops, Basil accused the second shop of doing just that – even to the point of getting business info from their employees.

WHEN THE FIRST STORE WILL ONLY GET HURT

The Pischei Teshuvah (156:3) distinguishes between when the second store will only hurt the first store and when it will put the first store out of business. He forbids the second type based upon the Chasam Sofer. The Chasam Sofer writes that even when the first store can support himself in some other way – it is still forbidden. This is also the view of the Masais Binyomin in a responsum (#27).

Rav Moshe Feinstein zt"l (IM CM 1:38) cites the Chasam Sofer and rules like him.

IS NEW YORK CITY AND ITS ENVIRONS ONE BIG MARKET PLACE?

Rav Yisroel Belsky zt"l once told this author of a ruling of Rav Moshe zt"l that in New York City and its environs, in many industries, it is considered like a shuk – a marketplace and restrictions on competition are not applied. There are many Poskim who subscribe to this opinion as well.

One must see a competent Posaik to determine the exact parameters of this view.

WHEN THE PUBLIC WILL SUFFER MAJOR ECONOMIC DAMAGE

There is another fascinating Ramah (CM 156:7) that states that if the first merchant's prices were significantly higher – then it may be forbidden to disallow the competitor. The nemukei Yoseph points out that the price differential must be significant. Otherwise what would happen is that each person would simply lower their price just a bit in order to permit it.

By the same token, if there is a large qualitative difference between the two products, Poskim do not necessarily disallow the competitor.

It goes without saying that the new competitor should never actively go after the first business's customers.

HORSE DRIVEN WAGONS VERSUS AUTOMOBILES

Rav Asher Weiss Shlita (Responsa Minchas Asher Vol. I #105) presents a fascinating point, and that is when the matter is of significant consequence to the public at large, halacha would never negate the public advantage for the economic benefit of the few business owners. Thus, he explains, Halacha would never forbid the development of motor vehicles in order to save the parnassah of the wagon manufacturers.

The Shalom Zachar – And the Shabbos Kiddush for Girls: Halachic Analysis

It is a minhag in Ashkenazic Jewish circles to host a Shalom Zachar where the baby is found on the Shabbos after a baby boy is born. It is generally held after the Shabbos evening meal. It is not a meal where people wash.

SEVERAL REASONS FOR THE MEAL

The Rambam (Hilchos Meulah 8:8) tells us that it is important to understand the reason why we do our Mitzvos. He also writes this in

Moreh Nevuchim (3:31). It is also the view of the Zohar (Parshas Yisro p. 93b) and Rabbeinu Yonah Shaarei HaAvodah #54. This is also true for understanding why we perform our customs. There are three reasons cited for this custom.

GRATITUDE REASON

The Terumas HaDeshen (Siman 269) explains that it is a Seudas Hoda'ah, a meal of thanksgiving. It is held in thanks that the child was saved from the travails and dangers involved in the birth. This is how the Terumas HaDeshen understands the view of Rabbeinu Tam cited in Tosfos in Bava Kamma (80a, "Yeshua HaBen").

This reason highlights to us the idea that we should always have and develop a feeling of gratitude and appreciation for all that Hashem gives us. We should also have this appreciation for all that others do for us as well.

APPRECIATING TORAH REASON

The TaZ cites another reason in the name of the Drisha. He writes that is based upon the Gemorah in Niddah 30b that states that when the child is born an angel strikes the baby on his mouth and causes the child to forget all of the Torah he had learned while in his mother's womb. This meal, according to the Taz is to mourn the Torah that was lost.

According to this reason, we highlight our appreciation for Torah study.

APPRECIATING SHABBOS

The TaZ provides his own reason based upon a Midrash found in chapter 27 of VaYikra Rabba. There, the Midrash explains why the Bris Milah is held on the eighth day. It draws a comparison between a king who tells his subjects that he will only grant them an audience after they first appear before a matronisa – a hostess. The TaZ writes that this is the reason we hold the Shalom Zachar on Shabbos.

From the TaZ we gain an appreciation of the gift that Hashem gave us in the Shabbos. It is important to remember that more than the Jew has kept Shabbos – Shabbos has kept the Jew. Although it is somewhat ironic that the person who coined this expression was not observant, it is, nonetheless, a truism.

WHY NOT FOR GIRLS?

Rav Yechezkel Landau of Prague is noted to have asked the question on the reason cited by the Terumas HaDeshen (in his Dagul Mervavah sefer on Yoreh Deah). If this is the, in fact, the reason for the Seudah to express our appreciation for the salvation of the baby – how come we do not hold this meal when a girl is born?

This author would like to answer that question with a shocking find. In Meseches Smachos Aivel Rabbasi (2:3) – we do find such a meal!

The meal is called "Shavuah HaBas" and it parallels the name found in Bava Kamma called Shavuah HaBen. It is also likely that the Kiddush that we have in shul on Shabbos when a girl is born is in order to fulfill this idea too.

It is well known that Rav Chaim Kanievsky Shlita has consistently advised young women who are still in search of a Shidduch to hold a Kiddush in shul – even if the girl is now in her twenties! It could very well be that the Shabbos Kiddush is a fulfillmeny of the "Shavuah HaBas" that is referenced in Aivel Rabbasi.

[This author is in the process of forwarding the question to Rav Kanievsky Shlita.]

REASON FOR THE NAME

The Yaavetz writes in his Sefer Migdol Oz that the reason it is called Shalom Zachar is on account of the fact that it is to remember or commemorate the Torah that was lost.

IS IT A SEUDAS MITZVAH?

The Trumas HaDeshen rules that, in fact, the Shalom Zachar is a Seudas Mitzvah. He cites as a proof that the Gemorah in Bava Kamma tells us that Rav entered the meal of Yeshua HaBen (as it was called then, according to the Trumas HaDeshen). We know from elsewhere (Chullin 95b) that Rav never ate at a Seudas Reshus – a festive meal that was not a seudas Mitzvah. Therefore, the Trumas HaDeshen concludes that it is a Seudas Mitzvah.

The Chavos Yair, however, disagrees. He states (Siman 70) that it is possible that Rav had just popped in and did not partake of the actual meal itself.

DELAYED BRIS

If the child is jaundiced or otherwise ill and the Bris will not be held within the next week, there is a debate among authorities as to when the Shalom Zachar is to be held. Some hold it on the Shabbos before the Bris (Yaavetz and Chochmas Adam 149:24), while others (Zocher Habris) hold that it is always the Shabbos after the baby is born. The language of the Ramah seems to indicate that he held to this view. The prevailing custom seems to be that it is held after the birth.

A FRIDAY NIGHT BIRTH

What happens when the baby is born on Friday night? In such circumstances it is often logistically difficult to arrange a Shalom Zachar. The Pri MaGadim (MZ YD 444:9) writes that one does it as close to the birth as possible. The Chayei Adaam, however, disagrees and writes that it should be done as close to the Bris Milah as possible. Each person should ask his own Rav.

Shabbos HaGadol – Why Shabbos?

To get some context, July 4th, 1776, was on a Thursday.

Imagine, l'havdil, if the founding fathers of the United States were to declare Independence Day as the first Thursday of every July rather than on the fourth of July. Everyone would ask the question as to why it was done this way – why on the day of the week rather than the day of the month? But, l'havdil, this is what we do on this Shabbos.

WHY NO DATE?

A great miracle happened on Shabbos HaGadol. Yetzias Mitzrayim, the Gemorah tells us, happened on a Thursday (Shabbos 87b). Therefore, the miracle that occurred on Shabbos happened on the tenth of Nissan. Most of the commentaries (Tur 430) tell us that Shabbos HaGadol is celebrated and called with this name on account of that great miracle that transpired on that day. If so, why was it established on the Shabbos before Pesach rather than on the tenth of Nissan?

THE ACTUAL MIRACLE

To understand the answer to this question we must first go back and understand what the miracle was exactly, in the first place. The Tur explains that there was a great miracle in that sheeps were worshipped as a deity in Egypt. The very fact that all of Israel took thousands of sheeps and tied them to their beds in preparation for a shechita and the Mitzrim said nothing to them – is a remarkable miracle. This is Rashi's understanding cited in Sefer HaPardes (page 343) and is also cited in Shibolei HaLeket (305).

Tosfos (Shabbos 87b "v'osos hayom"), however, bring down a different miracle. The firstborn of Mitzrayim asked the Bnei Yisroel while they were taking the paschal lambs why they were doing so. They responded that it was an offering in appreciation for the fact that the firstborn of Mitzrayim were to be destroyed. Frightened, the firstborn of Mitzrayim returned to their fathers and to Paro to let the Jews go. When they did not, there was a civil war in Mitzrayim erupted, decimating Mitzrayim.

WHY SHABBOS?

Both the Levush and the Prisha (Siman 430) explain that the miracle happened on account of Shabbos observance. How so? The Mitzrim only asked the Jews about the paschal lambs because of their observance of Shabbos. The Prisha explains that the Mitzrim did not know that Jews are allowed to tie a temporary knot on Shabbos and thus posed their question.

The Maharal MiPrague explains that it was Shabbos itself which had caused the miracle. Shabbos is a testament to the Oneness of Hashem and that He had created the world. Shabbos is the great antidote to

Avodah Zara and in her zchus the Mitzrim were unable to do anything to the Jewish people.

The Mogain Avrohom writes that the day that Miriam was to pass away was on the tenth of Nissan (See SA OC 580:2) – therefore that date was not chosen.

Bitul Chometz – A History and Overview

According to Torah law, we can dispose of our Chometz before Pesach either by Blur—destruction or by Bitul—negation. By Rabbinic law, we must do both. We are all familiar with the text, we recite it in the evening after the search for Chometz, and again in the morning while we burn it.

What is perhaps shocking is that no where in the Babylonian Talmud is this formulation found. There is certainly an obligation to annul the Chometz, but it seems from the Gemorah (See Psachim 6b) that this is a thinking process that did not necessarily have to be verbalized. The Ramban actually rules that one does not require a verbal declaration (See Ramban, Psachim 7a, 31b[1]). The Jerusalem Talmud (Psachim 2:2), however, states just the opposite. There, Rav is quoted as ruling that one must recite the formula "All Chometz that is in my house that I am not aware of shall be annulled."

The Rosh and the Rif, however, explain our Gemorah as stating that the annulment does require an actual verbal formulation. They differ slightly as to the verbal formula. There are actually four changes:

1] The first change is that the entire formula is no longer in the clear Hebrew that we find in the Jerusalem Talmud. The formula is now in Aramaic.

2] Another change is that the words in my house are now changed to in my domain.

3] The wording "that I am not aware of" is also changed to "That I have seen or have not seen, that I have destroyed or have not destroyed."

4] In addition, the Rif adds the words "shall be annulled like dust" while the Rosh adds "shall be annulled like dust of the earth."

Where did these changes come from and who made them? The Rishonim all point to the previous generation of Torah scholars – the Gaonim.

The reason for the first change is the subject of debate. The Ramah in his Darchei Moshe writes that it was for masses of people that were not fluent in Hebrew. During the times of the Gaonim, Aramaic was the prevalent language understood by all. Rav Yosef Teomim, however, in his commentary on the Mogen Avrohom cites the Ohr Zarua as stating an entirely different reason. The Gaonim were concerned with the effects that destroying bread, upon which man subsides, could have upon people. Had the annulment of bread been stated in Hebrew – an important language, the import of bread in the eyes of the people would be diminished. [As a parenthetic note, This explanation underscores the remarkable sensitivity and appreciation that the Torah desires us to develop within ourselves.] The Vilna Gaon adds that Chamira is not merely an Aramaic translation of the Hebrew term Chometz, it encompasses both Chometz and Seor[2].

There is another reason cited for the change to Aramaic. The Eliyahu Rabbah cites the reason that the Mazikim – negative spiritual forces – would understand it in Hebrew and would attack. We thus recite it in Aramaic so that they will be unaware of it. [One could perhaps ask that the Zohar in Parshas Trumah 129b indicates that negative spiritual forces do understand Aramaic, too].

The second change simply extended the boundaries of what the formulation applied to. Now it was no longer just limited to the house but included the Babylonian office buildings and ancient camelpacks (somewhat akin to the modern car trunk).

The third change clearly adds the incompetent burners on the morning of Erev Pesach who mess up on destroying the Chometz. They mess up by either not taking the bread out of the foil or including too much Chometz or simply not attempting to burn it thoroughly.

The fourth change perhaps more vividly illustrates to the reciter of the formula what annulment actually means. The Gaonim could have felt that the term annulment may have been too abstract a concept to the average Jew and thus provided a more detailed and vivid understanding of it by including the words like dust or like the dust of the earth.

Another question that exists in regard to the annulment is whether the Bitul can be annulled through a Shliach, through a messenger. The Baal Halttur holds that since a messenger is like the person throughout the entire Torah, a messenger can annul the Chometz of someone who sent him. The Rashba, the Ritva and the Nimukei Yoseph disagree and write that the actual owner of the Chometz must be the one who annuls it. The TaZ rules in accordance with the lenient opinion and states that someone who does utlize a messenger to annul, in all probability, has a reason for it. He is concerned that he may become busy or simply forget to annul it. His father-in-law, the Bach, however, was stringent.

From a drasha point of view, we know that Chazal explain that Chometz also represents the specific Yetzer HaRah of consumption. Perhaps the Rabbinic requirement to perform both Bitul and Biur can reflect the idea that we need every tool possible in which to battle this Yetzer HaRah. We should work to destroy the proclivity toward it within us. There is also another approach. We should ignore and negate it too. In this manner we can achieve the true freedom inherent in the Pesach holiday as defined by the Alter of Slabodka, the freedom from the slavery of consumptive desires to do that which Hashem truly desires of us.

[1] However, the Ritvah understood his Rebbe the Ramban that he also meant an actual verbal declaration is required. Rav Dovid Bonfid, another student of the Ramban understands his Rebbe in its simpler implication.

[2] Seor is actually, little known in our baking circles, but it was a leaven that was kept by bakers and added to the dough to cause it to rise. Now we just simple use pure yeast.

In Search of the Historical Pharoah

THE OBLIGATION OF VIEWING OURSELVES

The Gemorah in Psachim (116b) informs us that, in each generation, we are obligated to view ourselves as if we actually left Mitzrayim. Indeed, in Michtav MeEliyahu, Rav Dessler writes that since time does not progress linearly, but rather travels in a carousel like circle, the 15th of Nissan of the year 2448 is actually the very same 15th of Nissan of our own year now. This is one of our obligations on the night of Pesach. This being the case, that halachically we must view ourselves as actually leaving Mitzrayim, in our mind's eye we should envision and picture the escape.

Let's give it a try. Before us, standing at the water's edge about to enter it, stands Nachshon Ben Aminadav. Behind us, on a chariot, Pharoah is leading his hordes of well-trained soldiers. They are rapidly catching up. Yes, it is Pharoah – the short, obnoxious leader of the Egyptians that dared to present himself as a god.

But who exactly was he? What was his name? What do we know about him?

THE SEFER HAYASHAR

In the 77th chapter of a work called Sefer HaYashar, which was first printed in Venice in 1525, there are details as to what his name was, and more about who he may have been. [Alter Bergmann published a more recent edition of it in Tel Aviv]. The author of this Sefer HaYashar is anonymous, and there seems to be a debate as to whether it was written in the times of the Tannaim or is a much later compilation.

So, what do we know about Pharoah according to the Sefer HaYashar? Well, apparently he took the throne at the age of twenty. His father, Melol, was sick for the last ten years of his life, but had reigned for 94 years. His name was Adikam Ahuz. In Egyptian, according to the Sefer HaYashar, Ahuz means short, and short he was. He was an Ammah and one half, exceedingly ugly, and had a beard down to his feet. [One perhaps could best picture him as one of the seven dwarfs a la Snow White, but with a crown instead of a nightcap]. The Sefer HaYashar states that his reign started in the 206th year of Israel's going down to Mitzrayim, so he reigned for four years.

It seems, by the way, from the Sefer HaYashar, that only his advisors and confidants appended the pejorative Ahuz apelation to his name [the modern equivalent of shorty]. His subjects called him Adikam.

IS IT RELIABLE?

Is the Sefer HaYashar reliable? Good question. Looking through the work, we do find some interesting tidbits of information that do not seem to have other parallels in our extant Midrashic ouevre. For example, Tzipporah, Moshe Rabbeinu's wife is described as being on par with the Imahos, Sara, Rivkah, Rochel and Leah. Rabbi Aryeh

Kaplan z"l does use the work in his Chumash, and there are many parallels in other Midrashim and Gemorahs. Let's assume that it is reliable.

Let's now ask another question. Secular historians have all the Pharoahs named. What is the secular name of Pharoah? It is possible to accept the secular name and the surrounding history as accurate without necessarily having to accept the secular chronology as accurate. If we follow the standard dating, of when the old Pharoah (Basya's father) died and a new Pharoah arose (See Shmos 2:23) which occurred in 2444, this gives us the figure of 1316 BCE. The Pharoah at that time was called Horemheb, according to secular historians.

The name of one of the cities that Klal Yisroel built was Ramses (See Shmos 1:11). It might be tempting to accept Ramses II as the Pharoah. But his secular dating is much later 1134 BCE. Nonetheless, the thesis presented earlier might be acceptable – that there was some sort of a mix-up in their dating, somehow.

If we follow the 166 year discrepancy (or 163 years according to Rabbi Aryeh Kaplan) then the Pharoah is Thutmose III, who, according to the secular calculation, reigned from 1490-1436 BCE.

THE PEPI POSSIBILITY

There is another possibility (which was also mentioned in a Jewish Action a number of years ago.) It seems that there was a Pharoah known as Phiops II or Pepi, who is mentioned by Manetho, an Egyptian priest from Heliopolis. Manetho compiled an Egyptian history under the patronage of Ptolemy I, entitled Aegyptika. It was written in Greek and finished c.271 BCE. It is now only extant in translation and is available to us in Josephus. According to Manetho, Pepi ruled from age six to age one hundred. Manetho's datings have been questioned by historians who claim that there was political gain for the Egyptian priest in extending the lengths. However, the account has been verified through an Egyptian papyrus discovered in 1822 and called the Turin Royal Canon. (See Alan Gardiner, Royal Canon of Turin. Griffith Institute, 1959) [Parenthetically, The Turin papyrus dates to Ramses II and mentions the names of all Egyptian rulers preceded by the register of the "gods" who ruled over Egypt before the Pharaonic era. It was discovered in Thebes by an Italian traveler named Bernardino Drovetti. Eventually it was donated to the Museo Egizio by the king of Sardinia.]

There is another advantage to this approach, since the Ipuwer papyrus is now remarkably on mark. The Dialogue of Ipuwer is an ancient Egyptian poem preserved in a single papyrus, Leiden Papyrus I 344. It is now housed in the National Archeological Museum in Leiden, Netherlands. In general there is a debate as to whether Ipuwer was just being figurative or descriptive. For more information see Stephen Quirke, Egyptian Literature 1800BC: Questions and Readings (London 2004). But the parallels to Yetzias Mitzrayim, as seen below, are remarkable.

2:5-6 Plague is throughout the land. Blood is everywhere. 2:10 The river is blood. 2:10 Men shrink from tasting – human beings, and thirst after water 3:10-13 That is our water! That is our happiness! What shall we do in respect thereof? All is ruin. 7:20 ...all the waters of the river were turned to blood. 7:21 ...there was blood thoughout all the land of Egypt ...and the river stank. 7:24 And all the Egyptians dug around the river for water to drink; for they could not drink of the water of the river. 2:10 Forsooth, gates, columns and walls are consumed by fire. 10:3-6 Lower Egypt weeps... The entire palace is without its revenues. To it belong [by right] wheat and barley, geese and fish 6:3 Forsooth, grain has perished on every side. 5:12 Forsooth, that has perished which was yesterday seen. The land is left over to its weariness like the cutting of flax.

3:2 Gold and lapis lazuli, silver and malachite, carnelian and bronze... are fastened on the neck of female slaves. 4:3 (5:6) Forsooth, the children of princes are dashed against the walls. 6:12 Forsooth, the children of princes are cast out in the streets. 2:13 He who places his brother in the ground is everywhere. 3:14 It is groaning throughout the land, mingled with lamentations.

There is also one more tidbit. According to the Seforno, the term "Tzefardaya" means crocodiles—not frogs. The Ipuwer papyrus mentions crocodiles coming out of the Nile left and right on a path of destruction.

The halacha of envisioning us being there is not just theoretical. It involves physical action as well. The Rambam writes (Hilchos Chometz UhMatzah 7:6) based upon the verse in Dvarlm 5, "And you shall remember that you were a slave in Mitzrayim" as follows: "In other words, as if you yourself were a slave and you left to freedom and you were redeemed." The juxtaposition of this Rambam with the next halacha gives us remarkable insight.

The Rambam writes, "Therefore when a person eats and drinks on this night he must lean in the manner of free men." In other words, it seems that the obligation of leaning is a manifestation of this biblical obligation of imagining and visioning that it was actually us. So this Pesach let us go through the extra effort of picturing it with even more detail. A short, unattractive Pharoah named Adikam Ahuz chasing us in a chariot.

Going Away? Pesach Hotels and Bedikas Chometz

There are a number of people that go away for Pesach. Often they leave earlier – before the night of Bdikas Chometz – the night of the 14th (this year, Sunday night). They may to family friends, or a hotel. The following is this author's views on the nature of the obligation of the Bedikah. Please consult with your own Rav or Posaik, however, for halacha l'maaseh.

EARLY BEDIKAH

The halacha is clear that if a person leaves his house within 30 days of Pesach he is obligated to perform a bdikah – a search for Chometz before he leaves and to destroy it as well (SA OC 436:1). The Mishna Brurah explains that from that point on, Chazal have placed that obligation on him. We do not place the ten pieces of bread when an early Bedikah is done. There are a few reasons for this, but the main one is that the ten pieces are done because of a concern of a Bracha Levatalah, which is not going to be made on an early Bedikah anyhow.

The Bdikah is not a perfunctory one – but must be in all the holes and cracks. However, a blessing is not recited on these early Bedikas. If it is possible to delay leaving his home until after he does the Bedikah on the night of the 14th – this is preferable. Indeed, even if he is nearby, it is preferable to do the Bedikah in his home. The reasons for this are two-fold (see MB 433:35):

1] It is preferable to perform a Mitzvah in its ideal time, and

2] that it is preferable to perform a Mitzvah with a bracha than without one. We see this from the Mishna in Trumos (1:6) where it states that one who is not clothed should not perform the

Mitzvah of taking off Trumah. The Ritvah (Psachim 7b) explains that a Mitzvah is more choshuv – important when a bracha is made on the Mitzvah.

If it is too much, one can sell and or rent a number of the rooms and leave just one or two rooms for himself in which to do the Bedikah. This is actually a debate between the Mekor Chaim and the Chasam Sofer (Siman 131) as to whether a place that one intends to rent or sell to a gentile is obligated in a Bedikah now. The Mekor Chaim holds yes, the Chasam Sofer holds that it does not. If possible one should try to avoid the issue by selling it to the gentile a day earlier, but when necessary, one may rely on the Chasam Sofer.

ARRIVING AT THE HOTEL ON THE NIGHT OF THE 14TH OR BEFORE

If he arrives at the hotel on or before the night of the 14th, he should perform the bedikah in the hotel room just like he would if it were his own home. If the hotel room is already very clean (hopefully the norm in the United States at least), then he should eat Chometz in the room so that the room will not be considered as a "room in which Chometz is not brought in" and to be able to recite a bracha (See MN 435:4). It is questionable whether the scattering of the ten pieces of Chometz alone would create a situation where the cleaned hotel room would require a bracha. The hotel guest's car should also be included in the Bedikah.

A flashlight may be used for the Bedikah, and the electric lights do not have to be turned off.

It is interesting to note that in the Pesach Kovetz Halachos (page 77), Rav Shmuel Kamenetsky is quoted as saying that the cleaning in the room is done so well that it is considered as a place that does not need a Bedikah. He is quoted, however, as ruling that if Chometz is eaten there, then a blessing is recited. It is unclear as to why a person shouldn't specifically eat there, since he would be performing it with a blessing – which is preferable. Perhaps his rationale is that one shouldn't eat before a Bedikah.

ARRIVING ON THE DAY OF THE 14TH – BEFORE THE TIME OF BIUR CHOMETZ

If he arrived at the hotel on the day of the 14th, there are some fascinating questions that come into play – and it may get a bit complicated.

OBLIGATION OF PROGRAM DIRECTOR

If the Pesach program directors had rented out the rooms themselves and are subletting the room to the guests, then the obligation of Bedikah falls on them on the night of the 14th if they had rented as of the night of the 14th. If the program directors actually did do the Bedikah – then there is no obligation on the hotel guest. The Bedikah on the part of the program director can be done by a messenger, but it cannot be done via a gentile.

REALITY CHECK – HIS OBLIGATION

It is this author's understanding that it is rare that the program director actually does or oversees a bedikah for all the rooms that he has rented. Thus, if the program directors did not do a Bedikah, or if the program directors and or hotel owners are either not Jewish or not religious, the obligation lies upon the hotel guest to perform the Bedikah on that day. The bedikah is done with a bracha, under these circumstances. If the room is very clean (the norm in the US) and it is still before the Zman Biur – then he should eat Chometz there and then perform the Bedikah with a Bracha (based on MB 435:4). If there is not adequate time to do this, he should perform the Bedikah without a Bracha or with just thinking Hashem's name and saying the rest of the bracha.

IF HE ARRIVED AFTER THE ZMAN BIUR OR ON CHOL HAMOED

If he arrived after the Zman Biur, and the program directors did not make a Bedikah – he still performs a Bedikah, but without a blessing. However, if he arrived shortly after the Zman Biur, he may still make a Bedikah with a bracha – if it is still before what would have been the Zman Biur according to the Vilna Gaon. During the year, we follow the halachic hour calculation of the Vilna Gaon, but on Erev Pesach we are stringent to follow the view of the Magen Avrohom. The Magen Avrohom calculates hours from dawn to star-out rather than from sunrise to sunset.

Have a chag kasher v'same'ach wherever you are!

Pesach Meat Recipes: A Halachic Analysis

"What? You're not serious are you? No pot roast? No steak? Not even baked chicken?"

"Yes, that's our custom. You can't eat anything roasted on Pesach because people might think that it's Paschal lamb meat.."

"Wait, you prepare meat in a pot. The Paschal lamb was roasted over a fire on a wooden spit! They are not the same."

"It doesn't matter.."

The above conversation has transpired for hundreds of years in Jewish families throughout the world. What is the story with roasted meats on Pesach? It is only forbidden during the first seder or at both sedarim? What about the day meals?

BOILED CHICKEN AND STUFFED CABBAGE

It is because of this that many, many families have stuffed cabbage, boiled chicken or tongue or ribs as the main course at their Pesach Seders.

Tongue is always boiled. The stuffed cabbage is without the rice, of course. Some serve ribs that are baked in a sauce. Ribs are always baked in sauce. These choices are not random. Many Poskim actually advise utilizing these dishes because they are well-known to be cooked rather than baked.

THE SOURCE OF THE PROHIBITION

The Gemorah in Psachim 53a states: In those places where it is the custom to eat roasted meats on Pesach, one does so. In those places where it is the custom not to eat roasted meats on Pesach – then it is forbidden.

The reason is that since the Korban Pesach is only eaten roasted and on a spit and without water – there were those who were concerned that when one eats roasted meat – people would assume it was the Korban Pesach and that they were eating Kodshim outside of the holy places.

They were stringent and forbade the consumption of all meats – even meats that would not have been eligible for a Korban Pesach.

When they accepted this stringency upon themselves – they did so for all of their descendants. Indeed, it is in regard to such matters that Shlomo haMelech said (Mishlei 1:8), "Listen my son to the admonitions of your father and do not abandon the Torah [customs] of your mother."

The prohibition is codified in Shulchan Aruch Orech Chaim (476:1). It applies to all meats as well as to chicken (476:2).

It is also for this reason that many people only eat the roasted shank bone during the daytime rather than at the Pesach seder at night.

ROASTED IN A POT

Nonetheless, there is great debate as to the parameters of the prohibition. The Aruch HaShulchan (OC 476:2) rules that it DOES NOT apply to meat that is roasted in a pot – even if there is no water present. There is, of course, a debate in the Gemorah (Psachim 41a) itself between Rebbe and the Chachomim as to whether or not meat roasted in a pot is permitted. The Chachomim write that it is permitted, while Rebbe holds that it is not. Nonetheless, the Aruch haShulchan writes that is only in regard to receiving lashes in preparing the Korban Pesach incorrectly that they argue.

Indeed, the Aruch haShulchan questions why it is that some of the Acharonim are so stringent when the issue only revolves around a minhag and not an actual halacha.

The Mishna Brurah, however, citing numerous acharonim states that even if it is roasted in a pot – it is still a violation of our custom and forbidden.

Notwithstanding the Aruch haShulchan's point, most Poskim rule in accordance with the Mishna Brurah, unless one has a specific family minhag to rely upon the opinion of the Aruch HaShulchan. As in all matters of halacha, one should check with one's own Rav or Posaik.

DETECTABLE GRAVY

Rav Shmuel Vosner zt"l wrote (Shaivet HaLevi Vol. IX #120:1) that even though if one adds water it is not halachically considered roasted – the masses of people still call that roasted. He thus recommends that one add an additional amount of liquid to the extent that it be easily seen that there is a gravy to it. It appears that this suggestion would work even according to the Mishna Brurah.

LOGISTICAL DIFFICULTIES

The downside of this suggestion is that, as many chefs know, the best meats are ones that are the softest. That is why some cuts are more expensive than others in that the more expensive cuts come from the parts of the animal where the muscles are not exercised. When meats are cooked with additional water, it usually causes the meat to be tougher.

A WORKAROUND

One workaround to the tough meat problem is to cook the meat on a low flame for a long time. Expert chefs explain that even though one has added outside liquids, this should keep the meat softer. [As in all matters of cooking, one should check with an expert cook or chef.]

WHAT ABOUT FRYING MEAT [or Chicken]?

Believe it or not, meat that is fried is also a debate. The response Pnei Mayvin #123 rules that it is forbidden. He bases himself on the Pri Magadim in the beginning of YD #87 – who equates frying with roasting. Others, however, rule that frying is considered like cooking and not like roasting and permit it. [The Pischei Teshuvah and the Darchei Teshuvah #87 both rule that frying is akin to cooking and not roasting.]

WHAT IF THE MEAT WAS FIRST ROASTED THEN COOKED?

The Mishna Brurah rules that if the meat was first roasted and then cooked, it is permitted. The Pri Chodosh and the Kaf HaChaim (276:4), however disagree with this leniency. Yet a third opinion differentiates between whether it was roasted yet still uncooked before the Yom Tov started. If it was not cooked by the beginning of the holiday, the Yam Yissachar forbids consuming it!

DAY MEALS?

The language of the Mishna Brurah is that our custom (among Ashkenazic Jews) is not to have even a pot-roasted meat on both nights of the Seder. Since he does not mention the day meals being a problem — it is clearly indicative that he allowed such meat during the day meals. Not so is the opinion of a number of Chassidisha Poskim.

CONCLUSIONS

The customs in Klal Yisroel are, indeed, quite numerous. One of the themes on Pesach is the fact that we have carried these traditions since our exodus from Mitzrrayim. The most important thing to do, therefore, is to follow the minhagim of one's family in this regard. In doing so, may we merit the geulah speedily in our days. Next year in Yerushalayim!

Finding Chometz Over Pesach

Where is that tenth piece? Did we hide ten or was it really just nine pieces?

It has happened in the past to families that would never thought it would happen to them. Whether in a drawer that wasn't checked properly, a sofa cushion that had something underneath, or a compartment in a toy that went unnoticed before, each year there are numerous stories where Chometz is found over Pesach. And the incidences happen both on Yom Tov and on Chol HaMoed.

The Shulchan Aruch (OC 446:1), of course, tells us what to do. If it is found on Yom Tov – it must be covered with a vessel so that the Chometz not be seen. It cannot be moved, of course, because of the issue of Muktzah. At night, after Yom Tov, it must be burned.

This is based upon the Gemorah (Psachim 7a), that tells us that if one finds Chometz on Yom Tov one must cover it with a vessel, and when Yom Tov is over one should burn it. The reason for this is that there would be no biblical Mitzvah to burn it over Yom Tov, and the burning would constitute a burning shelo l'tzorech for no Yom Tov need. Why is this so? Because, presumably, he had already recited the formula for the Bitul, the negation of ownership of all Chometz big and small, hidden or revealed that he may own. Since he had already recited this Bitul formula, the Mitzvah of burning the Chometz does not set aside the laws of Yom Tov. [The Mishna Brurah rules according to the opinion of the Ran that burning it on Yom Tov would be biblically prohibited.]

WHEN ONE DID NOT SAY THE BITUL

There are two opinions, however, in a case where the person did not recite the Bitul formula. The Vilna Gaon rules that the halacha of the Shulchan Aruch applies across the board, and one may not destroy it or move it on Yom Tov. Other Poskim (Rashi, Rashba, SmaG, Ohr Zaruah), however, hold that when the Bitul was not recited, one may flush it down the toilet, throw it in a river, or scatter it in the wind. Which view do we follow? The Mishna Brurah states that the custom is like the first view, however, in a community where the custom is to flush it down the toilet through a gentile then one should not negate a custom in Israel.

IN CONTEMPORARY TIMES

The Shulchan Aruch ruled that, aside from issues of Yom Tov, if found – the Chometz should be burned even if one did recite the Bitul. However, things may have changed since then – in light of how we sell the Chometz in contemporary times. In our times, the forms in which we sell the Chometz include all Chometz that we own, known and unknown. What are the implications of this development? The

Chometz that we find therefore belongs to the gentile! If that is the case, is it then permitted to burn the gentile's Chometz?

This issue has been addressed by contemporary Poskim – Rav Tzvi Pesach Frank zt"l held (Mikrai Kodesh Vol. I Pesach #74) to the position that the Chometz should be placed in the Goy's section. Rav Shternbuch and Rav Wosner (Shaivet HaLevi Vol. IX #116) both hold that it is permitted to burn it. Rav Shternbuch bases his view on a Shach (CM 358:1) that If one is completely sure that his friend would be amenable to it, one may consume fruits without the permission of the owner. In our case, since the one who finds the Chometz is completely sure that the gentile would be amenable to the burning of the Chometz that was found, and that he would not have to pay for the balance of it after Pesach, it would be permitted.

HANDLING THE CHOMETZ

May one handle Chometz that is to be burned or should it be kicked to the site that one will burn it in? The Shulchan Aruch rules (446:3) that if a gentile's Chometz blew onto the roof of a Jew, he should move it with a stick but not handle it with one's hands. The reason is that when one handles things with the hands it is likely that one can come to eat it.

The answer is that one may touch it. The Mishna Brurah 446:10 states that since one is burning it one may handle it by hand if it is for a short period of time. It is a good idea, however, to say out loud that one is not acquiring the Chometz. This is based on a responsa of the Rivash cited in the Biur Halacha. Why is this so? Because a person's hand acquires items for him even if he does not have in mind that he is acquiring it.

Hopefully, however, most of us will have done a good job eliminating the Chometz before Pesach has started and there will be no need to be doing so on Pesach itself.

Nursing versus Bottle-Feeding: A Halachic Analysis

It is perhaps the issue that causes the most stress in regard to having a newborn child. Every parent wants what is best for their child. Yet sometimes, the difficulties and issues involving nursing are remarkably difficult to overcome. According to "The Informed Parent", a research based best-selling book that incorporates the latest science on parenting, of those that began exclusively nursing their baby, only 19% are still doing so at six months. Clearly, these mothers need a strong support system, from husbands, to parents to in-laws as well as the general community around them. The support must be extended regardless of the decision.

In a 2004 survey of more than 500 mothers, over half agreed that "women are put under pressure to nurse their babies. 44% of those surveyed said that women who bottle feed are made to feel guilty about it.

What follows is a halachic discussion of three different areas. The first is Onaah – causing emotional pain to another. The second is the general obligations to provide support to others, and the third area are the Mitzvos involved in the matter – especially regarding the current medical studies.

ONAAH

There is a verse in VaYikra the import of which has been little understood. The verse is velo sonu Ish es amiso – Do not afflict one another" (VaYikra 25:17). The Mitzvah is generally called "Onaas Dvarim" or just plain "Onaah." At times, making someone feel guilty about a decision can be a violation of this verse.

The violation is a very serious one. It is a Mitzvah that has also, somehow, fallen off the wayside. There is another prohibition called Onaas Mamom – monetary abuse. The Talmud (Bava Metziah 58b) quotes three sages who explain how the prohibition of Onaas Dvarim is by far more serious than the prohibitions of monetary abuse.

"But, we are doing this only to help!"

True, but nonetheless, it can still be a violation.

The Midrash Rabbah (Bereishis 14:19) explains that Menashe, Yoseph's son was punished for "finding" the goblet in Binyamin's sack – even though he did so on his father's instruction. He caused the Shvatim pain, they ripped their clothes in agony over the fate of Binyamin. The Midrash explains that Menashe's portion of his inheritance was also ripped.

Rachel Imeinu, stole the Teraphim of her father Lavan. Her intent, of course, was absolutely proper – also only to help. She wished to wean her father off of his belief in worshipping idols. Yet the Zohar tells us (VaYeitzei 164b) that she did not merit to raise those whom she loved because she deprived her father of what he loved!

EVEN THROUGH INACTION

As an aside, the Chikrei Laiv (YD Vol. III #80) writes this prohibition could also be violated through inaction. For example, if someone recites a Mishebarach for a number of people but purposefully leaves one person out – he is in violation of this prohibition. A sad aspect of this prohibition is that violators are often unaware that that they are verbally abusing or causing pain. Often they may characterize the recipient of their statement, words or actions as "overly sensitive."

Sometimes, there is a very thin line between proper parenting and Onaas Dvarim. This thin line must be navigated very carefully. At what point, do the comments turn from constructive parenting into a Torah violation of Onaas Dvarim? Often, people do not get the message unless the issue is made clear to them in no uncertain terms. Since that is the case, the issue is very pertinent – at what point is it Onaas Dvarim and at what point is it constructive criticism or constructive parenting?

The answer to this question depends upon the person's response. The Torah in many places stresses the obligation for one to be intelligent, and to be able to accurately assess likely responses of people. This situation is no different. An accurate assessment of the person's likely response must be made. If it is unlikely that a change will be effected, then further pressing the issue would be a violation of Onaas Dvarim.

IF ONE VIOLATES IT

What if one violated this prohibition? What must he do? The Talmud (Yuma 87a) tells us that there is an obligation to try to placate him – to undo the damage.

SUPPORTING THEIR DECISION

It is a Mitzvah incumbent upon every individual to love every member of Klal Yisroel, as it says, "v'ahavta l'rayacha kamocha." Included in this mitzvah is showing support for another – especially when they need it. Anything that you would want others to do for you in Torah and Mitzvos you should do for them.

Indeed, the Meforshim explain that this Mitzvah applies in three areas: monetarily, physically, and spiritually. The Bialer Rebbe Shiurei Mevaser Tov Bava Kamma page 14 writes that by far the highest level of this is in building someone up spiritually and being supportive of him or her. This is, indeed, reflected in the verse (Yishayahu 41:6), "Ish es rayahu yaazoru ul'achiv yomar chazak – They help each other and say to their companions, 'Be strong!'"

BENEFITS OF NURSING

Notwithstanding all of the above, there are remarkable benefits to nursing, and to doing so exclusively. Four months of nursing reduces the risk for respiratory infection hospitalization by 70%. Any nursing at all reduces ear infections by 25%. Any nursing at all reduces GI infections by 50%. It also reduces the risk of SIDS by 50%.

Going the extra yard, if possible, is a fulfillment of numerous Mitzvos in a better way.

There is a biblical mitzvah of taking safety precautions, as the verse states, "V'nishmartem me'od l'nafshoseichem" (Devarim 4:15). Cleaning the bottle and using hot and sterile water also fulfills this Mitzvah.

Hashavas Aveidah. The verse in Parashas Ki Seitzei (Devarim 22:2) discusses the mitzvah of hashavas aveidah, returning a lost object, with the words, "V'hasheivoso lo," "and you shall return it to him." The Gemara in Sanhedrin (73a), however, includes within its understanding of these words the obligation of returning "his own life to him as well." For example, if thieves are threatening to pounce upon him, there is an obligation of "V'hasheivoso lo." In other words, this verse is the source for the mitzvah of making the effort in saving someone's life. It is highly probable that it is to this general mitzvah that the Shulchan Aruch refers in Shulchan Aruch Orach Chaim 325. Both forms of feeding fulfills this Mitzvah.

'V'chai Achicha Imach.' The She'iltos (She'ilta #37), based upon the Gemara in Bava Metzia 62a, understands the words in Vayikra (25:36), "v'chai achicha imach," "and your brother shall live with you," to indicate an obligation to take steps to have others live with you. The Netziv in his HeEmek She'eilah understands it as a full-fledged obligation according to all opinions. Both forms of feeding fulfill this Mitzvah

BOTTLE FEEDING ALSO FULFILLS THESE MITZVOS

It should be noted that bottle feeding a baby also fulfills these Mitzvos as well, but nursing fulfills these Mitzvos in a slightly better way. We must recall, however, that we should never try to advocate a fulfillment of a Mitzvah in a better way if it will lead to causing someone Onaah – pain. Regardless, the Mitzvah of v'ahavta l'rayacha kamocha directs us to support whatever way they choose.

An Irreligious Sandek: A Halachic Analysis

It is a tradition among many Jewish people that the child at a Bris Milah develops, in personality, to be like the Sandek that held him at a Bris Milah. This is perhaps another motivation as to the reason why an attempt is made to obtain a great Tzaddik to serve as the child's Sandek. But from where did this idea originate? And what should someone do who has irreligious parents or grandparents and wishes to honor them with being Sandek?

The Ramah (YD 264:1) writes that a person should get a Mohel and a Baal Bris (i.e. a Sandek) who is yoser tov (very good) and a Tzaddik, a righteous person. It is unclear to this author whether the term "very good" as it applies to a Sandek is in terms of capability or in terms of moral character.

THE LEVUSH

The issue, however, is clearer elsewhere. Rabbi Mordechai Yoffe (1530-1612), author of the Levush, (Yore Deah 264:1) writes: "A person should take measures to find a Mohel and Baal Bris (i.e. a Sandek) who is a good and righteous in order that they have the highest and loftiest of intentions in their kavana and it will cause that the child will be like them." We see then that good means that it affects the child.

The original source of the Ramah is the Ohr Zaruah (Hilchos Milah 107). The Ohr Zaruah was written by Rav Yitzchok Ben Moshe of Vienna (1200?-1270?). Rav Yitzchok was a member of the Chassidei Ashkenaz and had studied under the Ra'avyah, Rabbi Yehudah HaChasid, the Sar mi'Kutzi and Rav Elazar Rokeach. He was also one of the Rebbeim of the Maharam M'Rothenburg.

A DIFFERENT REASON

In the Ohr Zaruah, the need for a good Sandek is for a different reason. It is so that they merit that Elijah the prophet will come. In other words, according to the Or Zaruah, it seems that it is not that the child will emulate the Sandek and or mohel – but that the greatness of the Sandek will effect the presence or absence of Eliyahu HaNavi!

The Maharil as well indicates that the issue is not one where the child will be influenced by the Mohel and the Sandek, but rather in terms of the health of child in his being additionally cured by the presence of Eliyahu HaNavi.

There is also the issue the Sandek is considered as one who has offered the Ktores. Indeed, in terms of receiving an Aliyah, the Sandek comes before the Mohel, if there are not enough Aliyos to give to both of them.

THE STRINGENT VIEW

Rav Moshe Shternbuch, in his Teshuvos v'hanhagos (Vol. I #603) is of the opinion that the irreligious person should not be offered Sandek, and that it could affect the child. He writes that the Mitzvah of honoring his father does not allow him to endanger his own son.

The Sefer Milah K'hilchasa questions this position on many grounds. At the end of the day, and although it is discussed in Shulchan Aruch, it is only a Segulah – not an actual halacha. He also does not see how a mere Segulah should set aside the Mitzvah of Kivud Av 'v'aim – honoring one's parents. Also, even in the Levush's own words we do not see that it affects the child negatively – we only see that a great person can affect the child positively.

THE OBLIGATION TO HONOR PARENTS

The Shulchan Aruch (Yoreh Deah 240:18, see also 241:4) discusses the obligation to honor parents – even where they might be evil-doers. Although the Remah does cite a dissenting view, that the obligation only exists after they have done Teshuvah, it is a debate. Many Poskim have stated that even according to the Ramah, when the parents have grown up in a situation where they may be considered a Tinok she'nishbah, like a child that was kidnapped and does not know better in terms of Jewish law – the qualification of the Remah – does not apply. [Regarding all of these issues, one should, of course, consult a Posaik.]

It is also well-known that the Chazon Ish (see Maaseh Ish Vol. II page 93) allowed a Shabbos violator an aliyah to the Torah. Rav Elyashiv zatzal ruled that a child who was raised in a manner where he did not know better and he does not observe Shabbos is considered as a tinok she'nishba, "kidnapped child," and may be counted in a minyan if he was not exposed to Torah. Thus, according to Rav Elyashiv, a yeshiva dropout may not be included in a minyan if he no longer observes Shabbos. But a Russian Jew, for example, who was not exposed to a yeshiva education can be counted (Peninei Tefillah citing Rav Elyashiv, page 127).

RAV ZILBERSTEIN'S VIEW

Finally, it is interesting to note that Rav Yitzchok Zilberstein, in his Chashuchei Chemed on Yuma (9b), suggests that one can honor an irreligious relative with being Sandek if he elicits a commitment from him to keep one Shabbos after the bris. The merit of observing the Shabbos, according to Rav Zilberstein, will more than make up for any possible drawback.

There is yet another indication that the approach of allowing it is perhaps preferable. Many Chassidic masters have recommended being a Sandek as a tikkun for certain Aveiros. If this is the case, then when there is a Mitzvah of honoring a parent or grandparent at hand, one should certainly do so. As in all matters of halacha, one should consult with one's own Rav or Posaik.

New Cars, Technology, and Sefirah

If you haven't bought a new car lately (or ever) – it's a whole new world.

Cruise control, for example, is now adaptive – it matches the speed of the car in front of you. Hondas now have drowsy driver detection as part of its optional Honda Sensing System.

There is automatic emergency braking with pedestrian detection. That means if a kid pops out in front of your car, it can automatically stop because it notices the kid on the bicycle befre you do. There is Apple-Play, that let's you safely use some features on your phone on the display. There is self-parking technology, and there are now internet hot spots in the car as well.

MAY ONE PLAN BUYING ONE?

All this new car technology, however, brings up the question as to whether one may plan to purchase a new car during the first 33 days of the Counting of the Omer.

THE SHULCHAN ARUCH AND THE MISHNA BRURAH

The Shulchan Aruch (OC 493:1) tells us that during this period it is our custom not to conduct weddings. The Mishna Brurah explains that one should not partake in matters of great joy. "Nonetheless," he writes, "if it happens that one has the occasion to recite a Shehecheyanu, then he may do so."

WHAT DID HE MEAN?

This sentence written by the Chofetz Chaim in the early twentieth century has developed a surprising amount of halachic literature over the years. What exactly did he mean by the term "if it happens?" Rav Nissim Karelitz (nephew of the Chazon Ish) in his Chut HaShani halachic work explains that the Chofetz Chaim means that one should not plan one's happy purchases to occur during this time. In applying his reasoning to our case, one should not at the outset plan to purchase a car during the Sefirah period. If, however, one's previous car has developed problems and a new car purchase is necessary, then, of course, one may make the purchase.

A DEBATE

Rav Chaim Kanievsky of Bnei Brak (cousin of Rav Nissim Karelitz) disagrees. He explains that the language utilized by the Chofetz Chaim here is "lav davka" not precisely worded. He writes that there is no problem at all in reciting Shehecheyanu blessings during the Sefira period. Rabbi Ben Tzion Abba Shaul zt"l and Rav Shlomo Zalman Auerbach zt"l also agreed with this reading of the Mishna Brurah.

THE STRINGENT OPINION

Not everyone, however agrees with the Mishna Brurah. The Divrei Malkiel as well as numerous other Poskim do write that one should avoid shehecheyanu's during this time. The custom of Klal Yisroel, however is to be lenient and follow the ruling of the Mishna Brurah.

THE TWO POSSIBLE BRACHOS

There is another issue too. Whenever we make a new and exciting purchase there are two possible brachos that may be recited. At times we recite a "Shehecheyanu" and at times we recite a "Baruch HaTov veHamaitiv." The Shulchan Aruch (OC 222:1; 175:4 and elsewhere) tells us that "Baruch HaTov VeHamaitiv" is recited when someone else also benefits from the item. A "Shehecheyanu" is recited when only one person benefits from the item.

Thus if two or more people are benefiting, which is usually the case when purchasing a family car, then the "Baruch haTov veHameitiv" is recited instead of a regular shehecheyanu.

Would this make a difference to the followers of either Rav Nissim Karelitz Shlita or those who have the stringent view?

Perhaps it might. The reason is that the words of the bracha of Shehecheyanu indicate an expression of thanks for having allowed us to reach this "special" time. The problem is that the tragic loss of the time may make this time period not so "special." Regarding the Three Weeks, the Mogain Avrohom (551:42) explains that the idea of not reciting a shehecheyanu is because of the wording, and not because of the idea of mourning. He writes, "However, the reason is not on account of mourning, for we do not find that a mourner is forbidden in reciting a shehecheyanu." Presumably, the same logic and may apply to the Shehecheyanu. Thus according to the Mogain Avrohom one may be permitted to plan to purchase a family car even at the outset.

Not everyone agrees with the Mogain Avrohom's contention that it is the Shehecheyanu that is the issue rather than the underlying purchase. The Maamar Mordechai, in fact, (also discussing the three weeks in 551:12) rules that the reason the blessing is not recited is, in fact, because of our mourning and pain. Rav Moshe Feinstein Zatzal discusses the purchase of cars during the Three Weeks in his Igros Moshe (OC III #80) and rules in accordance with the aforementioned Mogain Avrohom and not the Maamar Mordechai.

LEASING IS NOT A PROBLEM

One final thought. Even for those who wish to follow the more stringent view of Rav Nissin Karelitz that the purchase cannot be planned at the outset, one may, however, decide to lease a car. After a lease one does not end up owning the car and therefore there would be no Shehecheyanu recited. The very low interest rates that are available now for new car purchases are currently a deterrent to the idea of leasing.

CONCLUSION

So who do we follow? What is the bottom line halacha?

It would seem that the majority of Poskim understand the Chofetz Chaim's words as permitting the purchase of a Shehecheyanu during this time and even permit the planning of making such a purchase during this time as well. It may, however, be too late to bake the keys to the new car purchase in the Schlissel Challah.

Artificial Wombs and Halacha

It is perhaps one of the most remarkable innovations in the history of fetal medicine. It is called the "BioBag" and for all practical purposes, it acts like an artificial replacement womb. It is predicted that this device, already successful with sheep, could in a few short years, bring premature human babies to term outside of the uterus.

This innovation is significant because extremely premature babies have very difficult and dismal outcomes. Prematurity is the leading cause of death for newborns. In the United States, ten percent of babies are born before they reach 37 weeks. Six percent are born at or before they reach 28 weeks.

Those that are extremely premature, in order to survive, require mechanical ventilation. They need medications and intravenous nutrition as well as fluids. Their organs are not fully developed, or they are stunted in their growth, and between one fifth and one half of them still suffer from very serious health issues. This BioBag will soon change all of that.

THE HALACHIC ANGLE

This is a remarkable development that we can all welcome. Our question, however is: What are the implications of this device on halacha? More specifically, would a child born of an artificial womb still require a Pidyon HaBen? If so, would the pidyon haben be held thirty days after the baby (or fetus) came out of the mother's real womb, or would it be held thirty days after it emerged from the artificial womb?

Believe it or not, the answer to this critical question may lie in a Tosfos in Kesuvos (folio 4b, "Ad").

WHAT IT IS ALL ABOUT

Before we get to the actual discussion of the halacha and its sources, let's get a view of what the artificial womb is all about.

It looks like one of those oversized zip-lock bag that Glad (a registered trademark) manufactures. There are tubes of blood and fluid that go in and out of the bag. Indeed, in the experiment that was discussed in this week's Nature Communications Journal, eight fetal lambs developed within the BioBag.

For a period of four weeks, the lungs and brains of these eight lambs actually grew. The fetal lambs sprouted wool. They opened their eyes. They wiggled. They learned to swallow within the artificial womb, or the Glad bags, whatever one wishes to call these devices. And what they are called may be a critical point in the eyes of halacha. Are they actually a womb? Or are they a glorified incubator or a Glad bag?

The lead author of the article is a fetal surgeon at the Children's Hospital of Philadelphia, Dr. Alan Flake.

He says "the point of developing an external womb is to give infants born months too early a more natural, uterus-like environment to continue developing in."

Does the BioBag's appearance look like a womb, a rechem, in halachic terminology?

No, it does not. However, perhaps critically, it contains the same key parts. The womb is a protective sac that protects the developing fetus from the outside world. And so does the artificial womb. The womb has amniotic fluid. The Glad bag, or artificial womb has an electrolyte solution that bathes the fetal lamb in a manner that is almost identical to the amniotic fluid. It also allows the fetus to circulate its blood and exchange carbon dioxide for oxygen.

The Gemorah actually discusses a second womb, and its halachic implications.

The issue of how one views an incubator was once brought up to Rav Elyashiv zatzal by his son-in-law Rav Yitzchok Zilberstein, ylct. Rav Elyashiv answered that an incubator would not be considered equivalent to a second womb, but is rather looked upon as a machine that aids the fetus in his recovery (See Chashukei Chemed, Bechoros 49a).

BIO-BAG IS DIFFERENT

But this Bio-bag would seem to be very different than an incubator. Here is why:

This device actually mimics the circulatory system that connects the mother to the fetus. Here, the carbon dioxide that is produced by the fetus is exchanged for oxygen – just like the mother does for the baby. The blood flows with just the right amount of pressure as well.

If an external pump would have been used, it could overload the baby's delicate system. Dr. Flake and his colleagues created a pumpless circulatory system which allows the baby's blood to flow without another pump.

In an incubator system used in a hospital's NICU (neonatal intensive care unit), which was what Rav Elyashiv zt"l was asked about, the incubator is open air.

This system is different. The bag and the artificial amniotic fluid protect the fetus from infection. Fluids flow in and out of the bag just like in the mother's womb. It removes waste and keeps the fetus's developing lungs bathed with fluid.

RAV FEINSTEIN'S VIEW

Rav Moshe Feinstein zt"l was asked once about artificial hearts, and he explained that the devices are considered as actually part of the person. The halachic significance of which is that they need to be buried along with body of the deceased upon his death. It can thus be argued that according to Rav Feinstein zt"l – something that takes the place of a womb may also be considered to be a womb from a halachic perspective. One Posaik had informed me that Rav Feinstein's view was that the heart-lung machine is also considered a halachic heart and would, technically speaking, also require Kevurah. It is just that others would need it as well.

PRESSING ISSUE

The author of the study, Dr. Flake, predicts that in three years' time they will be ready to test the device on human beings. That being the case, the issue should be presented to leading contemporary Poskim as to what to do, because this may soon become normative medicine.

SOURCES

The Gemorah in Chulin 70a discusses the law of a firstborn animal. It states as follows:

What is the law if a person joined up two wombs [of two different animals] to each other and the fetus went from one womb and entered the other? Do we say that it exempts only its own [from the law of Bechor] but it does not exempt that of another [animal] or perhaps it exempts also that of another animal?

The Gemorah concludes that these questions remain undecided.

While some might say that the Gemorah's case may be different since although the fetus is taken out of the first womb and placed in a second womb, at least the second womb is a womb. Here the "second womb" is a plastic bag.

It can, however, reasonably be argued that the second womb, vis a vis the animal, is not substantially different than the BioBag under discussion. Since the Gemorah concludes that the issue is undecided – it would seem that, if our Poskim would consider this a Safaik – we should, in fact, either perform two Pidyon HaBen ceremonies – one thirty days after it emerges from womb #1 and the second one after it emerges from the BioBag. Or perhaps we can just do one Pidyon HaBen after "the second birth."

IS THE BABY EXEMPT ON THE FIRST BIRTH?

The Gemorah in Bava Kamma (11b) explains that if the firstborn is born as a treifa – it will not live – it is exempt from the need to redeem it. One could conjecture that an extremely premature baby should therefore be exempt from Pidyon HaBen altogether. However, Rav Yitzchok Zilberstein Shlita in his Chashuchei Chemed there explains that when the doctors state that the baby can live – even on account of technology, we do perform a Pidyon HaBen.

CONCLUSIONS

It is this author's view that the BioBag might very well be substantially different than the case of the incubator presented to Rav Elyashiv, and thus may be considered the second womb of the baby as in the Gemorah in Chullin. The Pidyon HaBen should therefore be performed 30 days after it emerges from the BioBag.

One last thought. The aforementioned Tosfos in Kesuvos states that the case of putting one womb next to the other and transferring from to the other was just theoretical and was discussed "lehagdil Torah ulehadira." Perhaps another interpretation of this concept is that Chazal were very much aware of future technological achievements and breakthroughs. This discussion, as we now see, is very pertinent.

Bugs in the Bathroom: A Halachic Analysis

It is a question that comes up every year when Yeshivos and Bais Yaakovs go away to summer camps for Shabbatones and Retreats. These retreats usually take place in May and June. The students are set up in bunk houses. True, the bunk houses are cleaned, but there is only so much that the cleaning staff can do.

THE QUESTION

The question is somewhat delicate, but since it is applicable to the laws of Shabbos – it needs to be discussed. One of the students uses the toilet, but unfortunately, a bug has lodged itself in the toilet. If one flushes – one kills the bug. If one doesn't flush, well, that is a breach in kavod habri'os – human dignity. What is the halacha?

THE PROHIBITION

The Gemorah in Shabbos (107b) tells us that the Torah forbidden Malacha of Shochait – slaughtering – even includes taking the life on an insect. However, we know that this only applies if one benefits from it, such as eating it or deriving some chemical from it. The Shulchan Aruch (Orech Chaim 316:8) clarifies that killing a creature with no benefit is a Rabbinic prohibition. That being the case, the aforementioned dilemma becomes applicable.

KAVOD HABRIOS

When it comes to matters involving human dignity, however, there are times in which the Poskim point to leniencies. The rationale is that the Rabbis did not create the prohibition when it would violate human dignity. This concept should only be applied by Poskim who are familiar with how and when to apply this concept.

DAYAN WEISS'S VIEW

Dayan Yitzchok Yaakov Weiss zt"l in his Minchas Yitzchok Vol. X #27 addresses this very issue and concludes that it is permitted based upon a number of factors: Firstly, the flushing is only indirectly killing them and the issue is that of Kavod HaBrios – basic human dignity. The actual killing of the insect itself is not being done for food or for its skin – it is therefore a Rabbinic prohibition alone. We can thus apply the rationale that under such circumstances the Rabbis never made their prohibition. Rav Vosner zt"l (Vol. VI #94) also rules permissively in such a case.

WHAT IF THERE ARE OTHER BATHROOMS?

We can distinguish between the cases where the bathroom was not yet used and the case where the bathroom was already used. When it was used already, one may still flush because it is not kavod habrios to leave the possibility of someone else entering and seeing an unflushed toilet. Even if it was not yet used, causing someone to travel or delay using the facilities is also a problem of Kavod HaBrios. Of course one should consult his own Rav or Posaik for these questions, unless of course it is too embarrassing to do so — in which case that too may be considered Kavod HaBrios.

One final thought. If there is a genuine concern for the zika virus in that area, or another dangerous disease, then most Poskim would permit killing a mosquito that has entered the house.

What Happens to the Soul After Death

Those who have suffered a great loss want to know what our Torah sources say about it, and it is a question that many ponder. Philosophers, scientists, and great men have explored this question since the dawn of time. What happens to the soul after death?

SOUL IS IMMORTAL

The Torah sources teach us that the soul is immortal. This is a foundation of Torah-true Judaism. This can be seen from the emphasis that is placed upon Shabbos observance. Although we keep Shabbos mainly because the Torah tells us to do so, it is also the flagship of Jewish belief. We stop all forms of creative acts because G d ceased and desisted from creative acts and rested on the seventh day. With our resting as well, we declare to the world that we believe in the Creator, that He is the essence of all that is good, and that He rewards good and punishes evil. In order to receive this reward and punishment, the soul must be immortal.

The neshamah, or soul, becomes attached to the guf, the body, while yet in the womb. The Talmud (Niddah 30b) derives this from the verse in Iyov (29:3) "When He lit His candle over my head; by His light I would go through the darkness." The Talmud further explains that the soul is taught the entire Torah during the nine months in the womb and that these days are replete with remarkable goodness.

The soul is likened to a lamp, as described in the verse "Ner Hashem nishmas ha'adam—a lamp of G d is the soul of man (Mishlei 20:27) and "For You light my lamp, Hashem; My G d brightens my darkness" (Tehillim 18:29).

THE SOUL DEPARTING

The Midrashei HaZohar on Koheles (p. 1196) explains that 30 days before the death of the person, the neshamah begins to fade away. However, it remains with the body until the moment of death, yetzias ha'neshamah. When the soul departs, it is compared to the extinguishing of a lamp (Shir HaShirim Rabbah 6:1).

The connection that binds the soul to the body is quite strong. The Gemara in Avodah Zarah (20b) tells us that in order to sever that connection, the Malach HaMaves, the Angel of Death, frightens the person to death, causing the soul to detach from the body. If the person had developed a close connection to Hashem in his or her lifetime, then there is ein macharid—there is no frightening on the part of the Malach HaMaves. Rather, the departing of the soul occurs because of its desire to attach to the Shechinah, which arrives as well.

The Megaleh Amukos (Parashas Emor, ofen 17) cites the Sefer HaTemunah, a Kabbalistic work, that when the soul departs the body, it sings the hymn of Mizmor Shir L'Yom HaShabbos. It is likely that this refers only to those on a high spiritual level. Such people merit to see

171

the Shechinah at the time that the soul departs (Avodas Yisroel of Rav Yisroel of Kozhnitz, Parashas Parah).

Sometimes the severing of the two is painful and sometimes it is not, depending upon the spiritual level of the deceased (see Ohr HaChaim Parashas Bechukosai 26 and Gemara in Berachos 8a).

The time when the soul departs is not insignificant. In Pirkei D'Rebbe Eliezer (34), it states that the sound of the separation is one of the six sounds that reverberates around the universe but is not heard.

THE FIVE FACETS OF THE NESHAMA

The Midrash (Bereishis Rabbah 14:9) refers to the general neshamah with five names or forces: Nefesh, soul; Ruach, spirit; Neshamah, breath; Chayah, life force; and Yechidah, unique singularity. The Master Kabbalists explain that the soul's five names describe five dimensions of the soul. Nefesh is the force that is the engine of physical life. Ruach is the emotional self, imbuing the individual with personality. Neshamah is the intellectual self. Chayah is the life force imbuing the person with will, commitment, and faith. Yechidah connotes the essence of the soul—its unity with its source, the singular essence of Hashem.

TIME OF CONFUSION

Immediately upon death, the neshamah can be in a state of utter confusion. It is thus considered a great chesed to remain with a dying person, so that he or she not die alone and confused.

During this time, the soul often forgets, out of a sense of confusion and fright, who it was. The Shla HaKadosh thus recommends that one become familiar with a verse in the Torah that alludes to his or her own name so that the soul can be calmed during this period. The verse alludes to one's own name if the first and last letters of the verse match the first and last letters of one's own name. These verses are usually found and recited in the back of the Shacharis Shemoneh Esreih.

The soul that is now detached from the body is painfully aware of any and all things that physically surround its body. This is particularly true before the body is buried. The soul can also hear words that are said by others that are around the body. The Talmud (Shabbos 152a) tells us that the soul itself mourns for its body for a full seven days. This is seen from the verse "His soul mourns for him" (Iyov 14:22).

It is for this reason that those who perform the taharah and those who watch the body before it is buried should refrain from frivolous conversation so that the neshamah not be further bewildered by what is transpiring.

The FIRST 12 MONTHS AFTER DEATH

For the first 12 months after death, portions of the soul hover over the body. For most neshamos, until the body reaches a certain level of decomposition, the soul wanders near the body and has no permanent resting place. This is one of the reasons for its pain and discomfort. The soul thus hovers over the body. During this time, the soul is aware of and is pained by the physical changes that occur to its body. Tehillim, praises recited to Hashem, are a source of comfort for the confused neshamah.

The Talmud (Shabbos 152a) therefore states, "Worms are as painful to the dead as needles are to the flesh of the living, as it is written (Iyov 14:22), 'His flesh grieves for him.'" The Mekubalim call this "Chibut HaKever"—punishment of the grave.

For some people, what happens to the body in the grave can be even more painful than Gehinnom itself.

JUDGEMENT

During that first year after death, the soul is initially judged by the Heavenly court. In addition to this initial judgment, the souls of the wicked are further reproved for 12 months after death. Others are reproved for a lesser time, depending upon the severity of what they had done and whether they have done teshuvah for it.

If teshuvah mei'ahavah, penance out of love of Hashem, was performed, then the sins that were done in one's lifetime are not only erased, but count as mitzvos. This is a remarkable "freebie" that is beyond our understanding. It also serves to lessen the amount of time that the neshamah spends cleansing itself.

Because those who are particularly righteous or who have done teshuvah mei'ahavah in their lifetime do not receive the full 12-month stay in Gehinnom, Kaddish is recited for only 11 months, in order that he not be judged as an evildoer.

Thus we see that if one is viewed positively here on earth, it affects, to some degree, the disposition of the individual in Heaven as well.

For this same reason, when mentioning a parent's name during the first year after death, one should say, "Hareini kaparas mishkavo— May I be an atonement for his resting place."

The main judgment after death is in Gehinnom, where the soul is cleansed in a spiritual fire and purified so that it can receive eternal reward. The fire abates every Shabbos.

SOULS SENT BACK

There are souls that are judged at the initial judgment as not yet ready for the spiritual purification that Gehinnom accomplishes. These souls are sent back to earth so that they will gain some sort of merit. When this transpires, then the process of judgment begins and then they can first get to Gehinnom. Even though, at times, this can take longer than the 12 months, we treat everyone as if they only have to do 12 months at most.

The souls of the righteous are quite lofty. They are, in one sense, even greater than the angels on high. How so? They are able to progress higher and higher in their ultimate heavenly venue. Zechariah the Navi was once told (3:7), "If you go in My ways . . . then I will give you a place to move among [the angels] standing here." Hashem showed Zechariah a vision of stationary angels, telling him that he would be able to move among them. Angels, having a limited form of bechirah— free choice—remain in one level of Gan Eden. A truly righteous person can move and ascend—both before and after the neshamah has departed.

MERIT FOR THE SOUL

How does this happen after the neshamah has departed? If, in one's lifetime, one left children that perform mitzvos, or one helped create Torah learning, or one has descendants or others who learn on his behalf, study Mishnayos on his behalf, or recite Kaddish on his behalf, he can shift his Heavenly station upward.

CONCLUSION

The Zohar tells us that out of the mitzvos that a person performs in his or her lifetime, the Holy One fashions clothing to place around the neshamah. These robes allow the soul to stand before the courtyard of the king. Without them, the soul cannot view the pleasantness of Hashem, Noam Hashem. The converse is also true. When aveiros, sins, are performed, a decrepit robe is placed over the neshamah and its judgment in Gehinnom then takes place.

The processes that occur to the neshamah after it departs from the body are complex and somewhat scary. Yet it is possible to prepare for this time properly. We see the tremendous importance of developing a dveikus, a cleaving to Hashem, of performing teshuvah out of true love of Hashem, and of supporting Torah study during our lifetime. May Hashem speedily bring about the removal of death laNetzach.

Tipping the Waiter: A Halachic Analysis

It was the young lady's third date. Her date had taken her to a restaurant to eat out. The conversation went well and he seemed to be a super guy. Shockingly, he did not leave a tip. To quote my seventh-grade daughter: "Awkward."

Aside from the question of what the young lady should do, another question arises. Is there a halachic obligation to leave the waiter a tip? What about tipping a taxi driver? Or an Uber driver? What is the halacha?

HISTORY OF TIPPING

From a historical perspective, tipping began as an aristocratic practice in England and then among the upper classes of Europe. After the Civil

War in the United States, wealthy Americans started visiting Europe in record numbers and brought back the custom to the United States to show off their worldliness. The New York Times in 1897 described the spread of tipping like "evil insects and weeds." In 1916, William Scott wrote an entire tract against tipping and called it the "Itching Palm." There he writes, "Tipping, and the aristocratic idea it exemplifies, is what we left Europe to escape."

Since then, however, tipping has become nearly universal in this country. This has some halachic repercussions. In less than a century, there may have developed a halachic obligation to tip based upon the near universality of the custom.

THE HALACHA

Generally speaking, the halachah is that payments agreed to in a transaction are what is binding. If no additional payments were agreed to, neither in writing nor orally, there is no obligation to pay it. However, the Rashba in a responsum (Volume II #168) writes that a minhag negates the halachah even in regard to monetary matters. This is true even if the issue was not specifically discussed either in written or oral communications prior to the contract. This is also the position of the Rivash (responsa nos. 171 and 474) and others as well. Indeed, local custom even in contracts is normative halachah. It is this author's view that in the United States, the custom has already developed to tip a taxi driver, but the custom has not (yet) developed to tip an Uber driver.

This is noteworthy because Uber drivers in New York City have gotten together and have formed a group called the Independent Drivers Guild. On April 17, this group successfully petitioned the New York City Taxi and Limousine Commission to create a rule that would require ride-hailing services such as Uber to add tipping capability into their phone apps. According to an article in USA Today, Uber has argued "since its inception that not allowing in-app tipping was one of the things its riders liked best about it." All this is proof that the custom to tip Uber drivers has not yet entered a state anywhere near of that which regular taxis receive tips.

The founder of the Independent Drivers Guild, Jim Conigliaro Jr., has said, "New York City's professional drivers have traditionally depended on gratuities for a substantial portion of their income. Cuts to driver pay across the ride-hail industry has made tipping income more important than ever."

Uber's major competitor, Lyft, has been attracting Uber drivers to come to their company because their app allows for tipping. This, too, is proof that tipping an Uber driver has not developed into the universal custom that the Rashba refers to.

Regarding tipping taxi drivers, the Debreciner Rav, z'l, Rav Moshe Stern, writes in Be'er Moshe (Vol. III #117) that if a chassidic-looking individual doesn't tip the taxi driver, it will cause them to avoid chassidic-looking people. He does not deal with the issue of universal custom, which would indicate either that he does not hold that it has become a universal custom in the United States or that he disagrees with the underlying application of the idea. But the fact that he writes that the taxi drivers would not come indicates that the concept of tipping has become universal.

MODERN POSKIM

The author of Ein Lamo Michshal (Vol. IX 16:8) writes that not tipping in a restaurant involves a "chashash issur gezel—a concern for the prohibition of theft."

However, that author's brother-in-law takes issue with this position (see Asher Chanan Vol. VII # 151) and writes that the former's position may be a chashash issur gezel on the rabbi's part for writing that there is an obligation to tip! Not to get into a possible family squabble here, it would seem that the real issue is how evolved the custom has become.

RAV ELYASHIV'S POSITION

In the Tammuz 5760 edition of the Mevakshei Torah Journal, Rav Elyashiv, zt'l, is quoted as saying that it is ch'shash gezel- there is a concern for theft if one does not tip at a restaurant (or at a wedding hall—where apparently the minhag has developed to customarily tip). He is quoted as saying that one must give a minimal tip.

Lest the reader think that this is merely a quote of Rav Elyashiv in a journal, Rav Elyashiv's son-in-law, Rav Yitzchok Zilberstein, shlita, writes (Tuvcha Yabiu Vol. II page 107) that this was Rav Elyashiv's view.

It should be noted that in Israel there is no minhag to tip taxi drivers, as opposed to here in the United States.

A POSSIBLE EXPLANATION FOR THE DEBRECINER RAV

A possible explanation of the Debreciner Rav z"l, who seems to have held that it is near universal to tip, but still did not consider it ch'shash gezel – possible theft is as follows: The person taking the job (whether a waiter or a taxi driver) knew that there is a tiny small minority of people that do not tip. They took the job or fare with this contingency in mind. Therefore, it may not necessarily be gezel – theft (Thank you B. Bodner for the explanation.)

HALACHIC CONCLUSION

To this author, it would seem that regarding taxis in the United States, there is a halachic obligation to tip. For taxis in Israel, there is no obligation. For Uber drivers, there is no obligation to tip as yet. Regarding waiters and waitresses in the United States, there would be an obligation. According to the author of Asher Chanan, however, matters have not reached the state where there would be any concern of halachic theft. As in all matters of halachah, one should consult his or her own rav or posek.

WHAT THE YOUNG LADY SHOULD DO..

Now let's get back to the awkward position of the young lady on the date. Saying something might cause the guy to feel bad, and she might violate the prohibition of ona'as devarim. However, there is also the issue of the other's halachic obligation. It would seem that she should delicately bring up the idea as a halachic discussion. If this is uncomfortable, she could feasibly rely on the poskim that permit not leaving the tip—especially if the issue was not mentioned by the Debreciner Rav in his responsum on taxis.

The Amazon Package that was left on the Porch on Shabbos

The package came on Shabbos. This time it was from Amazon Prime, but in the past it has been from Target.com or even Walmart.com. May one bring the item in the house? May it be kicked into a safe area? Or must it remain on the porch?

The answer as to whether or not one may bring it into the house, of course, is that it depends.

The answer as to whether or not one may kick it into a safe area is a Machlokes. This latter question we will address at the end of the article.

THE PACKAGE

It depends upon two factors, the package as well as the area. If the package is inherently Muktzah, the recipient is out of luck. Electronic devices, for example, are all Muktzah, as well as expensive items that we are super careful about.

TECHUM ISSUES

Assuming that the package is not inherently Muktzah, the Mishna Brurah (307:56) rules that the fact that they came from outside the Techum does not, by definition, make them Muktzah. We see in Hilchos Yom Tov (OC Siman 515) that even though one may not benefit from something that was brought to him from beyond the Techum – it is not necessarily Muktzah. How so? Because another Jew may benefit from it.

Letters, however, are a different story. The Mishna Brurah rules that if it is a letter that merchants would generally file away for safekeeping – then it is considered Muktzah. By the same token, any check or bill, or other business communication would be considered Muktzah.

What about one's Seforim order? Poskim have ruled, with some caveats that will be discussed shortly, that if one was aware of them beforehand and thought about them – one can actually learn from them on Shabbos! (See Kochvei Yitzchok Vol. II #18). If one didn't think about them, it is a debate among the Poskim, but if someone is lenient – we don't rail on him.

IF THE SENDER KNEW IT WOULD COME ON SHABBOS

The Mishna Brurah (515:68 and 72) rules that if the sender did not know that it would arrive on Shabbos or Yom Tov then on may benefit from the package. If the sender knew, however, one may not benefit from the packages contents until after Yom Tov – and one must wait until the time it would have taken to arrive!

IF THERE WAS A DELAY IN THE DELIVERY

Sometimes Amazon will blow the on-time delivery. Is it permitted to benefit from it then? The Shulchan Aruch (OC 515:9) rules that in such a case it is also not considered a problem – even for the person for whom it was sent.

READING NEWSPAPERS ON SHABBOS

Both the Mishna Brurah (307:63) as well as the Aruch haShulchan (307:9) pretty much forbid reading newspapers on Shabbos on account of business matters that are found in them. This is their position notwithstanding the lenient view of Shvus Yaakov (Vol. III #23, who permitted it on account of saving asset during wartime), the Maharsham in his Daas Torah (OC 307) and the Sh'eilas Yaavetz (Vol. I #162). The latter permitted it based upon the fact that there is enjoyment during reading it.

WHEN SUBSCRIBING TO A NEWSPAPER

When one initially requests a subscription to a newspaper there is an obligation to state that one does not want it delivered on Shabbos (See Maharam Shick OC 123).

What if the newspaper was actually printed on Shabbos? The underlying issue of course is melacha performed on behalf of Jews.

The Shmiras Shabbos K'hilchasa (31:24) writes that if the majority of subscribers are Jewish – it is entirely forbidden to be read. If the majority of readers are gentiles one can read the news section, but not the business section. However, every G-d fearing individual should avoid reading a newspaper on Shabbos. In footnote #70, Rav Shlomo Zalman Auerbacj zt"l is cited as holding that technically, one can assume that the extra papers that were printed on behalf of the Jewish subscribers were only a grama and that one can perhaps assume that the newspaper that he may be reading were form the majority that were printed for the gentiles.

NOT HANDED TO HIM

Getting back to the Amazon package, if the gentile has brought the package or letter from beyond the Eiruv, the Jew should not accept the package from him. The issue here is that of carrying. How so? Part A was the Akirah, the lifting up of the object from one domain, accomplished by the gentile when he began his route beyond the Eiruv. Part B is the hanacha the placement of the item that the Jew is now accomplishing. The correct procedure is to show the gentile where it may be placed.

MAY ONE KICK IT INTO A SAFE PLACE?

Now let's get to the final issue: May one kick the Amazon package? This is a Machlokes between the Mishna Brurah (311:30), who permits it, and the Chazon Ish (47:12), who forbids it.

The Chazon Ish reads the Rosh (Shabbos 3:19) as only permitting the indirect movement of straw with one's body instead of one's hands because it is not a detectable moving. Kicking, the Chazon Ish argues, is quite detectable, and therefore it would not be permitted.

The Mishna Brurah reads the Rosh differently and thus permits other body parts moving the Muktzah (See 308:13 and 308:30). The Shmiras Shabbos K'hilchasa (22:36) sides with the Mishna Brurah on this debate.

Of course, one should always check with one's own Posaik or Rav, but it seems that one may kick it inside the house if it is actual Muktzah.

Meeting With the Pope: A Halachic Analysis

Recently, Rabbi Edgar Gluck, his son Rabbi Tzvi Gluck, Rav DovBer Pinson, and a number of other prominent Orthodox individuals and Rabbis met with the Pope to discuss a number of important issues to the Jewish community. These issues included arranging proper kevurah for some unyet buried victims of the holocaust.

The meeting caused turmoil among some who believe that this was a misguided effort and that, in fact, it is forbidden to meet with the pope. To back up their point, some referenced various writings and responsum from both the Lubavitcher Rebbe ob"m and from Rav Moshe Feinstein ob"m. Nowhere in the responsum that were quoted, was there any indication that there is a prohibition in meeting with the

Pope for a legitimate concern. Indeed, the animadversions that Rav Feinstein was referring to involved joining up Jews and Catholics together in some sort of joint religious venture. It is true, however, that teh Lubavitcher Rebbe seems to be attacking people who have run after the Pope unnecessarily, but it is unclear as to the exact context of what he is referring to. There were many times in the past when people sought audiences for unnecessary reasons. One of the Rabbis here, however, was Lubavitch and it is likely that he sought guidance from Lubavitch Rabbis as well.

What follows, however, is an analysis of this topic.

Meeting with the Pope for matters of shtadlanus has been accepted practice in the Chassidic world, in the Litvish world, and in the Sephardic world since time immemorial. But first we will discuss the various Torah Mitzvos that are fulfilled in this type of Shtadlanus.

HASHAVAS AVEIDAH

One basic Mitzvah is that of saving lives. As we will see, this was the major motivation in meetings with past popes. What is the source of this Mitzvah? The verse in Parshas Ki Taytzai (Dvarim 22:2) discusses the Mitzvah of Hashavas Aveida – returning an object with the words, "Vahashaivoso lo – and you shall return it to him." The Gemorah in Sanhedrin (73a), however, includes within its understanding of these words the obligation of returning "his own life to him as well." For example, if thieves are threatening to pounce upon him, there is an obligation of "Vahashaivoso lo." In other words, this verse is the source for the Mitzvah of saving someone's life. It is highly probable that it is to this general Mitzvah that the Shulchan Aruch refers to in Shulchan Aruch Orech Chaim 325.

LO SAAMOD AL DAM RAYACHA

There is a negative Mitzvah of not standing idly by your brother's blood as well. This is mentioned both in Shulchan Aruch (CM 426:1) and in the Rambam. Clearly, in the post Crusades world and after World War II, this was the motivation.

LO SUCHAL LEHISALAIM

There is yet another negative commandment associated with the positive commandment of Hashavas Aveida, and that is the verse in Dvarim (22:3), "You cannot shut your eyes to it." This verse comes directly after the Mitzvah of Hashavas Aveidah. The Netziv (HeEmek Sheailah) refers to this Mitzvah as well.

V'CHAI ACHICHA IMACH

The Sheiltos (Sheilta #37), based upon the Gemorah in Bava Metziah 62a, understands these words to indicate an obligation to save others with you. The Netziv in his He'Emek She'ailah understands it as a full-fledged obligation according to all opinions. He writes that he must exert every effort to save his friend's life – until it becomes Pikuach Nefesh for himself. This was clearly the motivation to meet with the pope throughout our history.

V'AHAVTA LERAYACHA KAMOCHA

The Ramban, Toras haAdam Shaar HaSakana (p42-43) understands the verse of "And love thy neighbor as yourself" as a directive to save him from danger as well. Although he discusses the issue of medical danger, it is clear that this is an example, and it would apply to danger from physical enemies as well. Even without the Ramban, however, it is clear that defending and protecting someone from danger is a fulfillment of this Mitzvah.

BAAL SHEM TOV

The Baal Shem Tov is cited in Chassidic works as encouraging the practice (See Niflaos HaRebbi #387) in an incident with R' Koppel. The maaseh is cited in numerous places (See, for example, Talpios Vol. VII p. 189, Toldos Rav Yitchok MiKemarnah p. 26).

Rabbi Abba Zions z"l, a brilliant Talmud Chochom, an exceptional scholar, and an Alter Mirrer whom I was close with, had written an introduction and biographical sketch to the latest edition of the Paneach Raza, by the Rishon, Rabbeinu Yitzchok Bar Rabbi Yehudah HaLevi. He writes how it was Reb Tzaddok haKohain's view that Rabbi Nosson Officialo had met and debated with Pope Gregory X in 1273.

Of course, Jewish leaders have been meeting with the pope long before then. After the First Crusade massacres, there were continued threats of violence against European Jewish communities. Jewish leaders met with Pope Calixtus II who consequently issued Sicut Judaeis in about 1123. In this document, Pope Calixtus II urged all European communities to protect their Jews.

Rabbi Dovid Rofeh D'pumis, author of Tzemach Dovid and a descendant of the Aruch, met with Pope Paul the IV and succeeded in convincing him to rescind decrees against the Jews. Indeed, he dedicated his sefer to Pope Sixtus the Fifth.

Moses Montefiore, apparently with full Rabbinic approval, attempted to meet with the pope to remove the blame on the Jews on the tombstone of Thomas. He was not allowed entry.

RAV HERZOG

In June of 1944, Rav Yitzchok Herzog attempted to meet with the Pope to prevent further Jewish casualties, but the pope refused to meet with him. After World War II, in Adar Alef of 1946, the Rav Herzog left Lod airport to meet eventually with the Pope (Pius XII). He was accompanied to the airport on his mission to save the Jewish children that were saved were to be found in Catholic orphanages and missions. Rav Yitzchok Herzog met with the Pope in the Vatican in order to arrange their freedom. Otherwise, no Catholic institution would have released them.

Unfortunately, the response was a rather cynical one. Pope Pius XII asked Rav Herzog to provide him with a list of names of the children.

The Lubavitcher Rebbe in Toras Menachem Sicha Vol. XI p. 161 seems to cite approvingly the story of Rav Shlomo Molcho who refused to return to the Catholic Church and died a martyr's death al Kiddush Hashem. He had met with the Pope, which the Lubavitcher Rebbe does not seem to view negatively.

Rav Yisroel Meir Lau as chief Rabbi of Israel also met with the pope in an attempt to retrieve the kailim of the Bais HaMikdash. Rav Ovadiah Yoseph met with the Pope as well, as well as his son Rabbi Yitzchak Yosef, the current Chief Rabbi of Israel.

VATICAN COUNCIL II

This author posed the question to several Gedolei Torah in regard to whether the Rabbis in the late 1950's and 1960's were correct in their efforts to get the Catholic Church to abandon anti-Semitic attitudes and teachings in what became known as Vatican Council II. The unequivocal answer was yes.

These people who met with the pope should be applauded for their efforts on behalf of Klal Yisroel.

The Pope's Cross and the Shlomo Carlebach Song

It was certainly a bizarre sight to see: Yes, that was the Pope was slightly gyrating to Shlomo Carlebach music at today's meeting between him and Rabbi Edgar Gluck, his son Rabbi Tzvi Gluck, Rav DovBer Pinson, and a number of other prominent Orthodox individuals and Rabbis. The meeting was proper shtadlanus. However, there are a few other questions that should be addressed.

1] Is the Pope's shesi v'erev considered to be Avodah Zarah?

2] Was it appropriate to sing the pasuk, "orech yamim asbiyaihu?"

3] Was the singing and dancing appropriate, and what about during Sefirah?

IS IT AVODAH ZARAH?

The fact is that the Catholic Church believes in and promulgated the doctrine of the Trinity, which would fit into the technical definition of Avodah Zarah. They teach that G-d is simultaneously three distinct hypostases or persons who are coeternal, coequal, and indivisibly united in One Being.

Professor Harry Austryn Wolfson, the first to head the Department of Judaic Studies at Harvard University, (a former student of the Slabodka Yeshiva) in his classic work, the Philosophy of the Church Fathers, went through every explanation of the Church fathers' understanding of the Trinity – and each of these explanations, according to this author's understanding, still would clearly be considered Avodah Zarah. The Rambam (Hilchos Maachalos Asuros 11:7 and in Peirush HaMishnayos) states that it is considered Avodah Zarah (See Frankel uncensored edition). And while there are those who read a more moderate view in Tosfos Sanhedrin (63b), the majority view of scholars who have studied this Tosfos is not in accordance with this reading.

THE RAMAH IS LENIENT

This does not, however, mean that the particular cross under discussion is Avodah Zarah per se. The matter seems to be a debate. The Ramah in Yoreh De'ah (141:1) cites a ruling of the Trumas HaDeshen (Siman 196) that a cross around the neck is not considered Avodah Zarah to forbid one from benefiting. This is based on a Mordechai in the third chapter of tractate Avodah Zarah citing the Raavyah.

THE SHACH IS STRINGENT

Nonetheless, the Shach (141:6) writes that the Ramah's view is only when one is absolutely sure that the cross was not actually worshipped. The Shach concludes with a most stringent view.

Yet, the Chochmas Adam 85:1 also states that a cross that is hung across the neck is not considered Avodah Zarah and is only a zikaron – a commemoration. He extends it to others that are not necessarily hung on the neck. It is not just the Chochmas Adam's view. The Kinyan Torah (Vol. I 54:5) rules the same way.

The Klausenberger Rebbe (Divrei Yatziv YD #45) at first questions the Shach but at the end forbids matters in accordance with the Shach's view.

SINGING ORECH YAMIM ASBIYAIHU

The pasuk and song under discussion implemented in this context and with the comments of the Rishonim – indicate a veritable approbation extended here – beyond mere bracha. There is no question that the current Pope is certainly one of the friendliest popes to the Jewish people and community that we can recall, but the issue of theologically negating the absolute achdus of Hashem is not one that one can give an approbation toward. Indeed, the conclusion that one would derive from the responsum of Har Tzvi (OC 85) and the Chelkas Yaakov (YD 54) in regard to theological hesitations involving Avodah Zarah would seem that one should not go to such distances.

MUSIC AND DANCING

Aside from the issues mentioned above, there is another issue of it being Sefirah – a time of mourning. True, we do permit haircuts when visiting dignitaries, but playing live music and dancing is not something that is generally done in papal audiences. The language of the Mogain Avrohom 493:1 indicates that it is a Minhag to refrain from doing so, unless it is a Seudas Mitzvah. Had it been a meeting with President Trump, one could conceivably find grounds to go against the Minhag cited in the Mogain Avrohom – particularly, since Sefardic Poskim do not have this minhag.

CONCLUSION

As mentioned in a previous article, actually meeting with the pope and developing good will with the pontiff is certainly worthwhile to pursue. The song and dance was, in this author's opinion, not something that should have been tacked on. Of course, it is likely that the askanim posed the questions to their Rabbinic authorities and Poskim, who may have felt that uder the circumstances of the issues being discussed with the pope – it was warranted. The fact is that Reb Tzvi Gluck's work is so important and is a matter of Pikuach Nefesh that it may indeed, trump many of these other issues – in order to get the message out. On the other hand, it could be that the message could have been made without the singing and dancing.

Off the Derech Kids and Pesach Sheni

Today is Pesach Sheni. And although many people make sure to eat Shmurah Matzah today, unfortunately, few people understand its internal message.

It is a message brought out by the Gerrer Rebbe – the author of the Chidushei HaRim. Rav Yitzchok Meir Alter (1799-1866) was the very first Gerrer Rebbe. He writes that this particular day, Pesach Sheni, is a tikun for those who are perceived as beyond the pale – "B'derech Rechokah" – in his words. They are outside the scope of assistance. To them, to those who could not develop the closeness and Dveikus to Hashem that was emblematic of Pesach is this second chance.

The Psukim in Bahaaloscha tell us: There were men who were impure of the dead, therefore could not make the Pesach Korban on that day.

They approached Moshe and Aharon on that day. Those men said to him, "We are impure [because of contact] with a dead person; [but] why should we be excluded so as not to bring the offering of Hashemin its appointed time, with all the children of Israel? Moshe said to them, "Imdu – Wait, and I will hear what Hashem instructs concerning you."

The Chidushei HaRim writes that Imdu does not mean wait – but rather it means imdu in Teshuvah and Tefillah. It is not too late, just stand and pursue these two Avodahs and Hashem will help you along the way.

The Chidushei HaRim writes that this is the day for the off-the-derech kids that are now in every single one of our communities.

Each community among us, whether it be chassidisha, litvisha, or modern orthodox, has children that have left the fold.

Look around. They are hanging out on the street corners, at the late night Dunkin Donuts – hechsher and sans hechsher, and worse. Much worse.

Those that the Chiddushei HaRim refers to have issues of self-esteem, serious alcohol consumption, and many are abusing drugs. Many OTD kids have tattoos and multiple piercings.

They are everywhere – on Ocean Parkway in Brooklyn, in Lakewood, New Jersey. They are leaving Williamsburg in droves. And their parents toss and turn at night worrying about them.

It is to the point where, to echo a Pesach theme – "ain bayis asher ain bo mais – There is not a home that has not been affected."

This Chiddushei HaRim is telling us that we need visionary leaders who can revolutionize what is not working with our systems. We need leaders who can fix things so that the off- the-derech children do not find solace in areas foreign to Torah. We need leaders to keep our youth enthused in their Yiddishkeit.

We must conceive of not merely a stop-gap measure, but something more. We must research what the largest risk factors are. We must develop and innovate programs, plans and ideas that will reduce these risk factors. We need to put our collective minds and our financial pocket books together. Torah society needs a comprehensive solution to address this ever widening problem.

Indeed, the Sefer Chasidim (308) explains that even if there is significant financial strain we need to create separate institutions for our different types of children.

True, there are the Rabbi Tzvi Glucks, the Avi Fishoffs of Twisted Parenting, the Rabbi Dov Silvers of Madraigos, the Rabbi Zechariah Wallersteins, the Rabbi Yaakov Horowitzs, the TOVA mentoring programs. But we need to support them and replicate what they do on a massive, massive scale.

We need an FDR social security program, a Marshall Plan. A GI bill.

We need someone to step to the plate, someone that can make a profound change that will effect and save generations. And we need to put our moneys where our mouths are.

We sweep all of this under the carpet and do not talk about it, but this issue, hands down, eclipses all others.

How can we attend gala Bar mitzvahs and weddings, Yeshiva dinners and functions while knowing that there are children out there that we have failed? We as a community must regroup and come up with a viable, palatable solution.

How can we not cry for thousands of holy mothers in Klal Yisroel whose every thought and prayer centers around her lost son or daughter?

And time is ticking. Let's not kid ourselves. One or two years in the off-the derech lifestyle almost guarantees a point of no return. Those that do make the trip back are few and far between.

Our Rabbonim, our leaders, and our wealthy askanim need to hear from us. They need to hear of the heartaches that we suffer. Our voices need to be heard so that this issue will be given the prominence that it demands.

We can all do something. We can create happier homes and happier classrooms. We need to reach out to the people we see and smile at them. Of course, there are a myriad of reasons as to why these things can happen, and we cannot chalilah ever be judgmental.

We need to be that resource, that Rock-of-Gibraltar that genuinely cares about the neighbor's child who has that missing or divorced parent.

We need to put our collective heads together to create tools, resources, and institutions that will address the issue of our ever growing lost brethren. This all needs leadership, direction, and vision.

These forgotten souls must be placed once again on our agenda. That is the theme of Pesach Sheni, according to the Gerrer Rebbe. Let's listen to its message.

An Overview of Sfiras HaOmer

What follows is an overview of some of the spiritual dimensions of Sfiras HaOmer followed by some of the pertinent Halachos. Aside from the actual Mitzvah of counting the Omer, the period of Sfiras HaOmer can be a bit confusing. The reason that it may cause confusion is that there are actually three aspects to it.

• There is the first aspect that it was the time that we transformed as a nation from a lowly spiritual state to our highest point of spirituality ever in our history.

• There is the aspect of the offering of the measure of the newly grown barley crop that was brought to Hashem as an offering in the Beis HaMikdash on the 16th of Nissan. The amount of the offering was called an "Omer" which was one tenth of an Aifa. An Aifa is the volume of 432 chicken eggs. So the Korban Omer is the volume of 43.2 eggs.

- There is the sad aspect of this time period that it is a period of time when the 24,000 students of the great sage Rabbi Akiva died tragically.

The Meforshim (See Rashash Siddur p. 1070) have explained that the first two aspects are actually tied into each other. The Korban Omer is made of barley, generally the feed of animals. On Shavuos we bring the Shtei HaLechem, food that is the exclusive domain of man. Thus the two offerings represent the transformation from a low spiritual state to a high point of spirituality. Others have further pointed out that the third aspect also ties into the first two in that the students of Rabbi Akiva, unfortunately, did not entirely fathom the full depth of the lesson of the spiritual apogee that the Shtei HaLechem offering represents.

The Rambam writes that it is a Positive Mitzvah in the Torah to count the Omer, as it states (VaYikra 23:15), "And you shall count for yourselves Mimacharas HaShabbos." The word "HaShabbos" means after the Yom Tov – Pesach. The Rambam (Hilchos Tmidim uMusafim 7:22) is of the opinion that at this time, even though we are in Galus and we do not have the Beis HaMikdash, the Mitzvah still retains its Biblical status.

Most other Poskim (see Beis Yoseph OC 489), however, believe that the Mitzvah is now only MiDerabanan. The Ran, the Rosh and Tosfos hold that since we no longer have the Beis HaMikdash, the Mitzvah is only of Rabbinic origin. The Mishna Brurah rules like this latter opinion. However, the Ramah writes that we must be concerned for the opinion that it is biblical, and that is why we are stringent in regard to these laws.

PERIOD OF TRANSFORMATION

During this period, with Hashem's help, the Jewish nation transformed itself from the second lowest level of impurity into becoming the Dor

Deah, the generation of knowledge. In short, they catapulted themselves into becoming the greatest generation that ever lived.

The Zohar teaches us that on account of this transformation of the nation of Israel, the days themselves were imbued with special qualities and capabilities. How can we take advantage of them?

Our general tools of becoming close to Hashem throughout the year involve the areas of Torah, Avodah and Chessed. This is through developing our connection to Hashem through studying His Torah, in our Davening, and through emulating Him with acts of Chessed. The spiritual "high" we feel after performing a genuine act of Chessed, such as engaging in Hachnasas Kallah, is, in actuality, part of the journey of Dveikus Bashem – connecting and cleaving to Hashem.

During the time of Sefira, we include an additional set of tools. The brother-in-law of Rav Shlomo Alkabetz was Rav Moshe Cordovera zatzal, or the RaMaK. He lived in Tzvas in the 1500's. In the RaMaK's Galus HaShechina (p. 116 Yudaikin Edition) we find how these tools may be used:

Each of the seven weeks of the Omer represents one of the seven attributes of Hashem. Each day in the week also has the qualities of the seven attributes of Hashem as well.

• The first week represents the attribute of Chessed or lovingkindness.

• The second week represents the attribute of Gevurah or strength. Thus, the first day of the first week represents the concept or notion of Chessed within the concept of Chessed. The second day represents the idea of strength within Chessed. Rather than to be ignored, this should be viewed as a rung of spirituality that one can ascend in one's own personal growth.

• The third week represents the attribute of Tiferes or glory.

- Then comes Netzach, consistency.

- Hod represents beauty.

- Yesod represents fundamentals.

- The last week represents the attribute of Malchus – regality.

The combination of each of these attributes, wherein the attribute of the day is an element of the attribute of the week, serves to catapult our personal growth and development in emulating Hashem and developing our Dveikus toward Him. Thus, on the eighth day of the Omer, according to the RaMaK, we should focus on achieving the strength of Chessed (Gvurah sh'bechessed).

ALSO INCREASING OUR SENSE OF APPRECIATION

The Midrash further explains that the Torah gave us this Mitzvah of bringing the Korban Omer on the 16th of Nissan in order to remind ourselves of the Omer of Manna that we received from Hashem – each day we were in the wilderness. This element of the Sfiras HaOmer, therefore serves to increase our Hakaras haTov to Hashem for sustaining us in the wilderness as He made us into His Torah Nation. It also serves as a reminder that Hashem will always love us and watch out for us.

GENERAL HALACHOS

One should stand up when both reciting the Bracha and counting the day of the Omer. One has still fulfilled the Mitzvah, however, if either or both were recited while sitting.

The ideal time to count is after Tzeis HaKochavim – when 3 stars come out. It is also ideal to count after Maariv (See SA 489:1-2), however, it is permitted to count even before Maariv (MA 489:7). This is true even on Motzai Shabbos.

If one generally waits until the 72 minutes of Rabbeinu Tam but is in a minyan that counts earlier – it is preferable to count with the minyan earlier than on one's own later (See Minchas Yitzchak Vol. VI #45). Some Chassidim, however, hold otherwise (See Klausenberger Rebbe, Divrei Yatziv Vol. II #215).

Ideally, one should avoid counting during twilight – Bain haShmashos (MB 489:14). If he did count during this time he has fulfilled the Mitzvah, but he should also try to count after Tzeis HaKochavim without a bracha.

If one forgot to count at night then one counts the next day without a blessing and then it is permitted to continue counting with a blessing on the next nights.

If one forgot to count at night and also forgot to count in the daytime then one may not count with a blessing on subsequent nights. One still continues counting because many Rishonim hold that he still fulfills the Mitzvah.

The Shla writes that it is proper to make every effort to count the Omer in a Minyan.

If one counted silently, one has not fulfilled the Mitzvah and must count again with a bracha.

If one accidentally informed another of the day of the Omer then one may not count with a blessing. The preferred response is, therefore, to say, "Last night was the eighth night of the Omer.."

If one counted the days but not the weeks, he has fulfilled the Mitzvah, and can therefore continue counting on the next evenings with a Bracha. If, however, he remembered (either that evening or the next day) that he did not count the weeks, he should count again without a blessing.

The Vilna Gaon's version of the counting has the term "Ba'Omer." The AriZal and most of the Rishonim had the version "La'Omer." Each person should follow his or her own custom.

Some have the custom to also count in the daytime to help those who either forgot to count or erred to continue to count with a Bracha (See Yam shel Shlomo end of Bava Kamma that this was the minhag in Eretz Yisroel).

Many Ashkenazic women have the custom to count with a bracha. According to the Bais Yoseph it is forbidden for Sephardic women to count with a bracha. However, if an Ashkenazic woman is overburdened with other responsibilities and believes that it is unlikely that she will be able to maintain the count throughout – she should not count with a blessing.

A woman may not be Motzi a man with the blessing.

Children should be taught to count the Omer with a blessing. If the child misses one night, the Chofetz Chaim (BH 657) indicates that he should no longer recite the blessing but should continue counting. Some Poskim disagree with this analysis so one should consult with one's Rav.

When LaG BaOmer Falls on Sunday– A Halachic Analysis

For those who just want the bottom line – the answer is "Yes." When LaG BaOmer falls on a Sunday, you can get a haircut on Friday (if you are Ashkenazi) after davening – even if its only the 31st day of the Omer. What about Thursday night? Most Sefardim, however, have to wait until Monday morning, in accordance with the view of Rav Karo. Also, what about if one missed the haircut on Friday? May he get on on Motzai Shabbos – Saturday night?

There is a fascinating Remah (in Orech Chaim 493:2) that tells us that when LaG BaOmer falls on Sunday, the custom is to allow getting a haircut on Friday on account of Kavod Shabbos. The Ramah seems to cite the Maharil as the source for this ruling. In fact, the parenthesis indicating the source – was not penned by the Ramah but rather by a later editor.

A MIS-TRANSCRIBED LETTER

Indeed, if one looks at the Maharil, one sees no such indication in his writings that this is correct. What then is the source? It comes from some place else – it comes from the Mahariv – not the Maharil. Apparently, there is a mis-transcribed letter that has entered into our Shulchan Aruch.

TWO EXPLANATIONS

Poskim and Gedolei HaRoshei Yeshiva have given two explanations for the ruling found in the Ramah.

THE "SLAP IN THE FACE" EXPLANATION

One explanation is that since one is shaving and getting a haircut on Sunday, and Shabbos is right beforehand, it seems to be a "slap in the face" to the Shabbos that one did not get a haircut for the holiest day of the week too. In other words, it is the comparison that would be drawn from the Sunday holiday to the gift that Hashem gave us – the Shabbos.

THE HOLINESS BEGINS EARLY EXPLANATION

Another explanation is that LaG BaOmer is actually a holiday, where the holiness of that holiday begins at Mincha on the previous day. One does not recite Tachanun, for example, on the Mincha that immediately precedes LaG BaOmer. Since this is the case, one would technically have been permitted to shave and get a haircut on Shabbos. The only problem, of course, is that it is a violation of Shabbos.

And herein lies our heter. Since it is forbidden to do so on Shabbos – the minhag is to permit it on the day before – so that it could be done for Shabbos. This is the explanation of the Mahariv's position.

IS IT IDEAL?

What is interesting to note is that, although the Ramah cites sources that it is the minhag to permit these haircuts, is it ideal?

Rav Elyashiv is quoted by one of his students, Rabbi Avrohom Hillel Weinberger, author of HaGaos VeHosafos (as cited in Ashrei HaIsh p. 430) that although it is permitted it is "not mehudar" and it is preferable, rather, to get the haircut on Sunday.

SHOCKING POSITION

This position comes as a shock to most people. How so? Well firstly, the Mishna Brurah does not mention at all the notion that it is "not Mehudar." Secondly, it has been the minhag of all Bnei Yeshiva to follow this ruling of the Remah – ostensibly not only because it was permitted, but because it involved issues of Kavod Shabbos.

DEBATE AS TO THE ACTUAL REASON FOR MINHAG

It is this author's suggestion that the issue is actually a matter of debate between the Poskim of yesterday and Rav Elyashiv zt"l. Rav Elyashiv might hold of the second explanation of the Mahariv – that we just do it on Friday because we cannot do it on Shabbos. The Mishna Brurah and the Gedolei HaRoshei Yeshiva who permitted it fully in the past would hold of the first explanation of the Mahariv that it is a bit of a Bizayon to Shabbos to get a haircut the next day, but not for Shabbos itself.

CHOFETZ CHAIM HELD OF FIRST ANSWER – RAV ELYASHIV THE SECOND

Regardless, all authorities agree that it is permitted to do so. Some say that one should precisely because of the issue of Kavod Shabbos – Rav Elyashiv holds that Ideally one shouldn't. This author would like to suggest that the Mishna Brurah's silence here, and his ruling elsewhere regarding Rosh Chodesh on Sunday indicates that the

Chofetz Chaim was not in agreement with the view of Rav Elyashiv here.

CONCLUSION

One can certainly shave and get a haircut on Friday this year (According to Rav Mordechai Bunim Silverberg, Rav Shteinman permitted it even on Thursday night). Kikar Shabbat reports that they have a ruling from Rav Chaim Kanievsky that it is permitted on Thursday night as well. We can extrapolate from what Rav Ovadia Yoseph writes regarding the Sefardic minhag of the 34th day of the omer (Yechaveh Daas IV #32) that he permits it only when one is unable to do so on Friday. Other Sefardic Jews wait until the morning after lag baomer. Some question the Thursday night heter, however. The OU Halacha Yomis reports that Rav Shmuel Vosner zt"l held that ONE MAY NOT DO SO on Thursday night (MiBais Levi, Nissan 5758 p.87 note 3). One should, of course, ask one's own Rav or Posaik as to whether they agree with the idea that the Chofetz Chaim's silence indicates that he disagrees with Rav Elyashiv's point that it is not Mehudar, and as to whether they are permitted to do so on Thursday night as well.

Also, according to Rav Elyashiv in Mishnas HaGRish page 196 – if one missed the Erev Shabbos opportunity, he cannot get a haircut on Saturday night. He must wait until Sunday morning after davening.

DANGER WARNING: Be Careful With that Haircut

As virtually every barber with a Jewish clientele knows, a number Jews will be getting haircuts for LaG BaOmer. But, if they are not careful, these Jews could be in grave danger of violating a Torah commandment. Regardless, whoever reads this article before their haircut and follows the instructions below – will fulfill a Torah Mitzvah.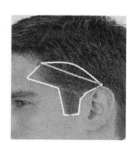

If you tell someone who is going to get a haircut about this Mitzvah – then you have been mezakeh that person with a Torah Mitzvah too. Oh, and one last thing. Reading it will help you avoid violating a Torah prohibition too.

209

TORAH MITZVOS REQUIRE INTENT

The Shulchan Aruch (OC 60:6 and 589:8) rules that when performing a Torah Mitzvah – intent (kavana) is required. The issue is a debate among the Rishonim, but the final halacha is that it does.

THE MITZVAH UNDER DISCUSSION

The verse in Vayikra 19:27 tells us, "Do not round off the corner of your scalp and do not destroy the corner of your beard." The halachos are codified in Shulchan Aruch (YD 181).

REASONS FOR THE MITZVAH

The Rambam writes (Laws of Avodah Zarah 12:1) that the prohibition is based upon the fact that idol-worshipping priests would cut their hair in this method. Thus the prohibition is based upon not following in the ways of idol-worshippers. The Sefer HaChinuch (251) and SMaG (Lav 57) present this reason as well.

The Tur (YD 281:1) indicates that it is a Mitzvah of which we are unaware of the underlying rationale, but we follow it because it is the commandment of the King.

INTENT FOR HAIRCUTS

The Kaf HaChaim (YD 232:15) writes that this is true for haircuts as well. If we have in mind that we are fulfilling the Mitzvah of "Lo sakifu p'as roshchem" – we receive credit for the Mitzvah. If we do not have this in mind, then we lose out on it. Bear in mind, that we should also have in mind the Mitzvah of Kavod Shabbos and the Mitzvah of Kavod Yom Tov.

WHERE ARE THE CORNERS?

Every Jewish man has two gun-shaped areas that pointed slightly upward that are located next to his ears. The best way to understand the parameters of where cutting hair on the head is forbidden is to imagine four parts of a gun: The muzzle, the barrel, the hammer and the bottom of the grip or the handle.

• The muzzle is the front – where the bullet comes out (A). It is where the hair starts coming down.

• The barrel is the long tube that leads to the back of the gun (B).

• The hammer is the back of the gun that faces the holder of the gun (C). It is the high point above the ear.

• And the bottom of the grip (D) is the lowest part of the gun. Regarding hair, it is the bottom of the side burn.

If you look at the picture you will see the outline of the gun's four parts.

It is this gun which forms the pe'ah of the head in which we cannot round off our hair. It is found on both sides of the head.

• The muzzle, once again, is where the hair starts coming down. Every man's muzzle starts off at a different place.

• Some are of the opinion that the barrel must be rounded and not straight as a precautionary measure.

• There is a debate as to whether the hammer is at the top point of the ear or slightly above it.

• There is also a debate as to where the bottom of the grip should end. Rav Feinhandler in Avneh Yashpeh (Vol. II #68) cites Rav Elyashiv zt"l as holding to the view that it should be at the bottom of the earlobe. The Chazon Ish (Orchos Rabbeinu page 20) held that the bottom of the gun grip is parallel to the lower point of the ear canal.

INTERESTING OTHER ISSUES

Approximately three decades ago, this author had a conversation with Rav Chaim Pinchas Scheinberg zatzal, who indicated his view that the gun extends to even behind the ear toward the back of the head too. His view is that there is one gun following another gun. Most other Poskim do not seem to hold of this view.

There has been a trend, of late, for people to leave the area of the gun more prominent whenever they get a haircut. Thus the area of the gun is much more prominent in that it is cut with a higher trimmer number.

WHAT IS FORBIDDEN?

Cutting hair in the gun-area short with either a razor blade, a shaver, a barber's trimmer, a scissors, tweezers and depilatory cream is forbidden (this is the Rosh's view [see Makos 3:2] that the Shulchan Aruch tells us to follow YD 181:3).

This means anywhere in the gun area. Even shaping or edging the gun area with a barber's trimmer is thus forbidden.

It is forbidden to cut the hair so short that it is no longer bendable. In other words the top of the must be able to touch the root of the hair. In Hebrew this is called, "Lakuf rosho l'ikro." These parameters can be found in Rambam Hiulchos Tumah (Tzaraas 8:10) and other Poskim cited in Minchas Yitzchok (Vol. IV #113). Rav Elyashiv zt"l's view (cited in Pe'as Ziknecha page 30) was that to fulfill all opinions it must be left a fifth of an inch long, or 5 millimeters. Generally speaking, a #2 shield leaves the hair bendable. A #1 does not – nor does a 1 and a ½.

COMMONLY VIOLATED

It is a sad reality, but it seems to this author that a majority of otherwise Torah observant people – litvish, chassidesh and sefardic are completely unaware of these three things. They do not know the exact parameters of where the forbidden area actually is (where the gun is), that the area around the gun cannot be trimmed, and they do not know how short the hairs within the gun may be cut. This information should be spread in order to prevent people from unwittingly violating Torah laws.

Is Lag BaOmer Really So Important?

The answer is a resounding, "Yes." Even though the Ramah (Shulchan Aruch OC 493:2) tstates that on LaG BaOmer we engage slightly in Simcha – joy, commemorating LaG BaOmer is a serious matter. The Mogen Avrohom cites the Kavanos HaArizal that discusses a certain individual who had the habit of reciting Nachem every day. He continued to do so on LaG BaOmer as well. For doing so he was punished. We see, therefore, that one should take the words of the Ramah quite seriously.

A number of reasons are cited by Torah authorities for commemorating Lag BaOmer:

• It commemorates the students of Rabbi Akiva who ceased dying during this day – although the deaths persisted between Pesach and Shavuos. (Shla Psachim 525).

• This day is the Yartzeit of Rabbi Shimon Bar Yochai who revealed the inner secrets of the Torah (Chayei Adam Moadim 131:11)

• This is the day that Rabbi Akiva granted ordination to his five students – among them Rabbi Shimon Bar Yochai – they did not die in the plague that struck Rabbi Akiva's other students (Pri Chadash OC 493)

• It also commemorates the Manna which began to fall on this day after the Bnei Yisroel left Egypt (Responsa Chsam Sofer YD #233 "Amnam Yadati").

In this short essay, we will attempt to discuss each of the four reasons mentioned above.

The Students of Rabbi Akiva

The Talmud (Yevamos 62b) tells us that 12,000 pairs of Rabbi Akiva's students died on account of the fact that they did not extend honor to one another. Rav Chatzkel Levenstein zatzal asks how it could be that the great students of Rabbi Akiva neglected this most basic of principles?

His answer is most illuminating. Our Rabbis teach us that Kinah, Kavod and Taavah – jealousy, the pursuit of honor, and the pursuit of desires take one out of this world. "If so," Rabbi Akiva's students reasoned, "how can we accord each other this spiritual poison?"

Rabbi Levenstein explains that they were unaware that, in fact, honor is only poisonous when one seeks it – but when one extends it to another it is not poisonous at all. When we build the self-esteem of others, it is actually quite healthy. Rav Levenstein explains that this notion is very subtle and nuanced and it could well be that the notion itself was only revealed in the world at that time. Why then were they punished? They were smart enough to have been able to figure out and contemplate this issue by themselves. Having neglected to delve into this psychological insight was their error.

Rabbi Shimon Bar Yochai

Rashbi, whose Yartzeit we commemorate on this day, merited to compose two extraordinary books that form part of the Zohar. They are the Adara Rabbah and the Adarah Zutah. Rav Yoseph Chaim in his Responsa (Rav Pe'alim YD #156) explains why it was that Rabbi Shimon Bar Yochai, above and beyond his masters the Tannaim, merited to write these extraordinary books. He explains that although his teachers and masters were greater than he was, he had the ability of couching these teachings in esoteric terms. Indeed, Rabbi Shimon Bar Yochai was so adept at obscuring the true understanding of these thoughts, that they could even be expounded upon publically – and only those that truly merit understanding it would be able to figure out the true inner meaning and import. According to this, we commemorate the fact that Rabbi Shimon Bar Yochai not only transmitted these remarkable teachings, but vouchsafed them in such a manner that they not be abused or taught to those who are unworthy.

Jewish Continuity

The ordination that Rabbi Akiva conducted on his five students was a heroic event that changed the course of Jewish history, and that of the world. These students were Rabbi Meir, Rabbi Yehudah, Rabbi Yossi, Rabbi Shimon and Rabbi Elazar Ben Shamoa. Under the pressure of the dark forces of Roman tyranny and religious oppression, these valiant scholars, who were privy to the noblest ideals of the Bible, its teachings and oral traditions, knew that no matter what the cost – they must ensure the continuity of these teachings. They were the future educators of us all.

It was a point in time where the forces of evil and darkness were pitted against goodness and light.

The light of Torah ultimately won out and Torah Judaism was to effect and alter the world. We commemorate this remarkable event on this day of LaG BaOmer. The words of the Mogen Avrohom concerning the man who was punished for not commemorating this day are, therefore, well understood.

The Manna

The Manna represents the spiritual nourishment that G-d granted the Jewish people upon their departure from Egypt. Manna allowed us, the Jewish people, to develop a close bond, a Dveikus, with the Creator – that has defined who we are as a nation. Although the Manna no longer falls, the admonition that the Jewish people have to continue that bond, to continue imitating G-d and attempting to be like Him has never ceased.

The Talmud (Shabbos 133b) tells us Mah Hu Rachum af attah Rachum veChanun – just as He is Merciful, so should you be merciful. Just as He is kind so too must you be kind. Just as He clothes the poor – so should you clothe the poor. Just as He buries the dead, so should you buy the dead.

This is the message of the Manna that still exists to this day, and this is what LaG BaOmer commemorates.

Nonetheless, perhaps due to the deaths of so many of Rabbi Akiva's students, the Minhag is to celebrate a little bit and not to make it into a full-fledged holiday. The Chsam Sofer points out that our Talmud does not mention it as a holiday at all.

So how do we commemorate this day? The Bnei Yissasschar states that the custom is to light a number of candles in Shul on this day. We do not fast on this day – even for a Yahrtzeit, except for a fast of a bad dream. We do not recite Tachanun on this day, nor on the Mincha before it. We get married and attend weddings. We join in with singing and dancing, and we listen to music (See Pri Magadim Aishel Avrohom 493:1).

So as we hear the song and dance of the Jewish weddings and the words, "Od Yeshamah, let it still be heard in the cities of Yehudah and in the outskirts of Jerusalem, the sound of joy and the sound of happiness, the sound of the groom and the sound of the bride" let us think of these four reasons: Building the self-esteem of others and according others due honor is of utmost importance; vouchsafing the teachings of the Torah is paramount; Jewish continuity and education is key; and the spiritual bond and Dveikus that we have with Hashem should be central to our lives.

May Hashem bring the Geulah Shleimah speedily in our days!

Mosquitoes and Halacha

To some they are very irritating and pesky. No, not the buzzing, whining, biting mosquitoes, but the neighbors whose habits somehow bring about mosquitoes. It is mosquito season, and the season brings on its own unique set of halachic issues – particularly when it comes to the laws of neighbors – hilchos sh'chainim.

By the way, here are a few tidbits about the small creatures. Due to one's body heat and carbon dioxide levels, mosquitoes can seek you out from up to 75 feet away. They are also attracted to the breath and sweat of human beings. They are also attracted to dark colored clothing much more so than light-colored clothing.

THE QUESTIONS

The questions abound. Is there a halachic requirement to empty the lid of a garbage can when rain water has collected in it? May a neighbor request of the other neighbor to avoid overwatering with the sprinklers – because it brings out more mosquitoes? Can one neighbor force the other to clean out her birdbath water? And what about swimming pools? Is there a halachic obligation to keep the pool water both treated and circulating?

SPRAYING CAUSES THE MOSQUITOES TO GO NEXT DOOR

Also, when one neighbor has his lawn sprayed, it often happens that all of his or her mosquitoes end up going to the neighbor's house and yard. Often when one sprays the lawn, the mosquitoes looking to escape actually enter one's own home and start biting away.

When this happens to a neighbor, is there any financial responsibility on the spraying neighbor's part to the one being damaged?

FIRST GROUP OF QUESTIONS

According to the EPA, mosquitoes undergo four stages during their life cycle. Three of these stages include being near or in water. Standing water increases mosquito reproduction. The questions about standing water and the obligations will thus be addressed first.

OBLIGATION TO PREVENT DAMAGE

There is, of course, an obligation to refrain from causing damage to one's neighbors or to others – even on one's own property. The second chapter of tractate Baba Basra deal with the obligation to engage in preventative measures to avoid damage. The first Mishna there states: "One may not dig a cistern next to the cistern of his neighbor, nor a water channel, nor a cave, nor an irrigation ditch, nor a washing trough – unless he distances it from the outside wall [of the neighbor's cistern] three handbreadths and seals it with plaster."

IMMEDIATE DAMAGE

In terms of a financial obligation, however, the halacha follows the view of Rabbi Yossi that it is the obligation of the Nizak, the one being damaged, to ensure that the Mazik – the damaging neighbor doesn't damage him. There is one caveat. If the person is standing in his property shooting arrows at his neighbor's back yard then he is completely responsible financially. In the Talmud's language (Bava Basra 22b) this is called "girei dilei – his arrows." This is codified in Shulchan Aruch (CM 155:31-32). The simple understanding of this is that it includes any action that causes immediate harm.

Therefore a neighbor can plant a tree near the ditch of his neighbor, because the tree will not cause immediate damage.

IF THE NEIGHBOR IS FELIX-LIKE

There is a fascinating halacha (CM 155:39) in the Shulchan Aruch that discusses a case where a person had permission to work with either animal blood products or animal skins in his own property. However, crows or ravens began to gather and track blood on the neighbor's fruits and they caused damage to him or made cawing noises that irritated him the neighbor. He must stop his activities. The Ramah adds that the same applies to any other significant type of damage that a person cannot stand. The Sma explains that the word "to him" indicates that the neighbor is excessively finicky. Even in such circumstances the neighbor must distance or cease his activity.

The Chazon Ish (Bava Basra 10:1) explains that the case of the ravens is likened to shooting arrows. It would seem that the mosquitoes would be no different than the ravens.

Therefore, although one should ask a shailah to one's own Rav or Posaik, it would seem that one neighbor can ask the other to:

1] Empty the lid of a garbage can when rain water has collected in it after it rains.

2] Request the other neighbor to avoid overwatering with the sprinklers.

3] Ask the neighbor to clean out her birdbath water.

4] Ask the neighbor to keep the swimming pool water both treated and circulated.

The Mishpetai Choshain (155:25) rules that the spraying neighbor does not have a financial obligation to pay, but he should inform the neighbor of the time that he will be spraying so that the neighbor can take appropriate actions to protect himself.

KILLING MOSQUITOES ON SHABBOS IN A ZIKA ZONE

Generally speaking killing mosquitoes on Shabbos is a violation of Shabbos. The Rambam holds that it is a biblical prohibition, while other Rishonim hold that it is a serious Rabbinic one since it is often aina tzricha legufo – there is no need for the dead carcass. However, if there is Zika virus in the area or during times when there is a serious concern for a fatal illness, it would be permitted to kill it. One should consult one's own Rav or Posaik, however. In New York at this time, there are no concerns that would warrant it.

When is the Best Time to Daven for Parnassah?

The members of Klal Yisroel are maaminim bnei maaminim, believers the children of believers. A vast majority realize that it is Hashem that brings us Parnassah, and not our own, "kochi v'otzem yadi." We just must perform our proper hishtadlus, and daven to Hashem for parnassah.

But when is the best time to make the request?

The answer? Amud HaShachar.

Rav Yonasan Eibeshitz (1690-1764) writes in his Yaaros Dvash (Elul first Drasha):

"They [the sages] have said in tractate Brachos 3b. When the dawn arose, the sages of Israel entered to King David and said to him: Your nation Israel requires parnassah..

It requires clarification as to why they came to him at the crack of dawn. The answer is that in the morning Hashem is filled with compassion for Israel, hen he sees that the nations direct themselves to their Avodah Zarah. Israel serves Hashem with all their heart. It is then that he sustains and provides for us.. And then the Holy One blessed be He is filled with Mercy. Therefore it states (Tehillim 90:14), "sabeinu baboker chasdecha – Satisfy us in the morning with Your Kindness." Similarly, while we were in the Midbar it was in the morning at dawn that we received a layer of dew.

The following prayer for Parnassah is found in the Sefer called Shaarei Dimah.

יְהִי רָצוֹן מִלְּפָנֶיךָ יְיָ אֱלֹהֵינוּ וֵאלֹהֵי אֲבוֹתֵינוּ, שֶׁיִּהְיוּ מְזוֹנוֹתַי וּפַרְנָסָתִי וּמְזוֹנוֹת וּפַרְנָסַת בְּנֵי בֵיתִי עִם מְזוֹנוֹת וּפַרְנָסַת כָּל עַמְּךָ בֵּית יִשְׂרָאֵל, מְכֻתָּרִים וּמְאֻמָּתִים וּמְצֻדָּקִים בְּיָדְךָ, וְאַל תַּצְרִיכֵנִי לִידֵי מַתְּנַת בָּשָׂר וָדָם וְלֹא לִידֵי הַלְוָאָתָם, כִּי אִם לְיָדְךָ הַמְּלֵאָה הַפְּתוּחָה, הַקְּדוֹשָׁה וְהָרְחָבָה. וּתְהֵא מְלַאכְתִּי וְכָל עֲסָקַי לִבְרָכָה וְלֹא לַעֲנִיּוּת, לְחַיִּים וְלֹא לָמָוֶת, וּתְזַכֵּנִי שֶׁלֹּא יִתְחַלֵּל שֵׁם שָׁמַיִם עַל יָדִי. וְאֶהְיֶה מִן הַמּוֹעִילִים וּמַשְׁפִּיעִים טוֹב לְכָל אָדָם תָּמִיד, וּתְמַלֵּא יָדִי מִבִּרְכוֹתֶיךָ וְשַׂבְּעֵנוּ וְשַׂבְּעֵנוּ מִטּוּבֶךָ, כְּמוֹ שֶׁעָשִׂיתָ לְיוֹצְאֵי מִצְרַיִם, כִּי אַתָּה יְיָ בֵּרַכְתָּ וּמְבֹרָךְ לְעוֹלָם. עֵינֵי כֹל אֵלֶיךָ יְשַׂבֵּרוּ, וְאַתָּה נוֹתֵן לָהֶם אֶת אָכְלָם בְּעִתּוֹ, פּוֹתֵחַ אֶת יָדֶךָ, וּמַשְׂבִּיעַ לְכָל חַי רָצוֹן. הַשְׁלֵךְ עַל יְיָ יְהָבְךָ וְהוּא יְכַלְכְּלֶךָ, לֹא יִתֵּן לְעוֹלָם מוֹט לַצַּדִּיק. וְאַתֶּן נְשָׁמוֹת הַקְּדוֹשׁוֹת וְהַטְּהוֹרוֹת, הַעְתִּירוּ אֶל יְיָ בַּעֲדִי וּבִגְלָלִי, יָרִים קַרְנִי וְיַגְבִּיהַּ מַזָּלִי, לְמַעַן אוֹכַל לְעָבְדוֹ בְּלֵבָב שָׁלֵם כָּל יְמֵי עוֹלָם אָמֵן

Sheitels From One's Own Hair

There are companies out there that specialize in making wigs (sheitels) from one's own hair.

Generally speaking, these companies do it for those undergoing chemotherapies r"l, but others are also doing it. These companies state that the hair needs to be healthy enough to withstand the hand tying process. They require a minimum of 8 ounces of hair in order to make a custom wig, and point out that the average woman has 3-4 ounces of hair on her head. The cost is about $1000 and the length of the sheitel is 3 inches shorter than the hair submitted.

Our question, however is not in regard to the cost or the process. Our question is what the halacha is regarding using one's own hair for a sheitel. Is it permitted, forbidden, or a machlokes?

A BRIEF HISTORY

Let's first take a look at the history of wigs before we get to our specific question. The human hair wig as we know it first appeared in ancient times, then virtually disappeared after the fall of Rome in 473 CE. It then reappeared in the last six centuries.

We find that the Egyptians wore wigs to protect against the hot sun. They attached the wigs to their head using beeswax and resin. The Assyrians, Greeks and Romans also used wigs.

The term wig, by the way, is short for periwig.

IN THE MISHNA

The Mishna in Shabbos (6:5) also attests to the use of wigs, and the Gemorah later on clearly shows that it was done for beauty. Both Rashi and the Meiri explain that it was worn so that "she would appear to be a baalas s'ar – having [much] hair."

Rashi in Bechoros (7b) seems to add more information. He writes (D"H nehenim b'saarah), "The women who had little hair used to attach (or tie) the hair of other women to their hair and this is called peah nachris."

THE WIG IN HALACHA

The Ramah (75:3) discusses the halacha of reciting the Shma in front of a woman who is wearing a wig. The Ramah writes that it is permitted to recite it. The Mishna Brurah explains that it is because he holds that this, the wig, is not considered "s'ar b'isha ervah. – the hair of a woman is forbidden." There is a view that is of the opinion that wigs are forbidden because they are still considered "the hair of a women which is ervah."

TWO VIEWS ON WIGS

Most Ashkenazic Poskim (See Igros Moshe Even HaEzer Vol. II #12) and families, however, followed the lenient opinion regarding wigs. Indeed, the Kaf haChaim (OC 75:19), Mishpetai Uziel (EH Mahadurah Tanina #74), and Yaskil Avdi (Vol. VII EH #16), all prominent Sefardi Poskim also permit the wig. On the other hand, Rav Chaim Palaji (Ruach Chaim EH 21) and Rav Ovadiah Yoseph zatzal (Yabia Omer V EH 5:4), however, follow the stringent view forbidding wigs for Sefardic women.

Rav Chaim Kanievsky Shlita stated that the Chazon Ish's wife wore a wig (cited in Meir Oz Vol. III page 829) as did his mother. He also ruled that if a Sefardi studied in an Ashkenazic Yeshiva he may allow his wife to wear a wig, otherwise, she should cover her hair with a kerchief.

All this, of course, relates to a wig with another woman's hair, but what about one's own hair?

WITH ONE'S OWN HAIR

The Mishna Brurah (75:15) cites two views in this regard. The first view he cites is that of Rav Yoseph Ben Meir Teumim (1727-1793), author of the Pri Magadim. The Pri Magadim is of the opinion that use of a Peah Nochris, a sheitel, is permitted. The Mishna Brurah then states that it is indicative in the language of the Pri Magadim that he permits the use of one's own hair in the manufacture of it as well.

THE STRINGENT VIEW

After quoting the Pri Magadim, the Chofetz Chaim then cites the view of the Mogen Giborim (written by the two brothers-in-law, Rav Yosef Shaul Nathanson [1808-1875] and Rav Mordechai Zev Ettinger [1804-1863] and published in two parts) who were stringent in this manner and forbade it.

It is also interesting to note that manuscripts of Rav Teumim have been found in the Bodleian Library at Oxford (1:1500:16419) of his work entitled "Aim LaBina" mentioned by R. Avrohom Meir Livshitz Breizel printed in 2014 which show that days before he passed away, Rav Teumim retracted his whole heter for wigs entirely. Nonetheless, we have a dictum that an author's more authoritative work will set aside a lesser work that he wrote, even if he wrote it later.

Rav Nissim Karelitz Shlita (Chut Shaini Shabbos III page 272) writes "praised be the one who, in her tznius, can fulfill the halacha according to all opinions." It is clear that Rav Karelitz Shlita believes that, ideally a woman should be stringent in accordance with the view of the Magain Giborim. What, however, is the view of the Mishna Brurah? What is normative halacha?

The earliest source who discusses the topic is Rav Yehoshua Boaz Ben Shimon Boruch (d. 1557) of Northern Italy, the author of the Shiltei Giborim. He writes on tractate Shabbos (64b) that the wig is permitted and it makes no difference whether it is her own hair or that of another woman. He also shows that this is clearly referring to a married woman because the Gemorah states that she wears it so that she not be found unappealing in the eyes of her husband.

The Levush, however, forbade the use of a person's own hair, disagreeing with the Darchei Moshe in (YD 303) who indicates that it is permitted. The Ateres Zkainim also understands the Ramah as permitting it with one's own hair.

THE BE'ER HAITEV'S VIEW

It would seem that the fact that Be'er Haitev does not even cite the more stringent view of the Levush is indicative that he holds the halacha is clearly like the Ramah – permitting it. This is borne out by the fact that in Even ha'Ezer (Siman 115) he just cites the view of the Shiltei Giborim without bringing any dissenting view which forbids it.

CONCLUSION

When the Mishna Brurah cites one authority and then a second one who is stringent, the general understanding that he rules in accordance with the first view (heard from my Rebbe zt"l, Rav Henoch Leibowitz zt"l – a relative of the Chofetz Chaim).

Also, generally speaking, the Pri Magadim is more authoritative than the Mogain Giborim. This combined with the view of the Shiltei Giborim would indicate that as a matter of pure halacha, notwithstanding the recommendation of Rav Nissim Karelitz Shlita, it would be permitted to use one's own hair.

However, the fact that the Mishna Brurah cites the view forbidding it as well – indicates that it is not being unduly strict to be machmir.

As in all matters of halacha, however, one should always ask one's own Rav or Posaik as to how to conduct oneself.

Dinner Honoree Ads, Chiseling, and Halacha

There has been, of late, a vast proliferation of Jewish organizations, dinners and dinner honorees. The proliferation of these three has in turn given birth to a new phenomenon called "Dinner Honoree Ad Chiseling." It goes something like this:

"Yes, I would like to put in a full page color ad for the honoree, but I can't pay the regular price."

"Okay look. I can give you the full page for $700 instead of $1000."

"No. Can't do that. I will give you $300 but you have to give me two seats too."

"Fine. But don't tell anyone."

"Sure."

THE PROHIBITION

The prohibition known as Gneivas Daas, is about fooling or deceiving others in physical practice. Is putting in a $1000 ad, but only paying $300 considered Geneivas Daas?

The Gemorah in Chullin (94a) cites Shmuel as saying that the prohibition applies to everyone.

The Gemorah in Chulin 94a cites a Braisah which discusses four examples given by Rabbi Meir of things that are forbidden on account of the issue of Gneivas Daas:

• It is forbidden to repeatedly invite someone to a meal when you know that he will refuse.

• It is forbidden to repeatedly offer gifts when you know that he will refuse.

• It is forbidden to appear to up a new barrel of wine (when one is actually opening it for a previous sale) unless one informs him of the real reason he has opened it [the underlying issue is that the wine will not last as long now that the barrel is open and it is a big favor to the guest, much like opening a brand new bottle of Blue Label would be nowadays].

• It is forbidden to offer someone oil from an empty flask to anoint oneself when one knows full well that the person will refuse it. If, however, he is offering the oil to show (others – Rashi) his fondness for the person it is permitted.

We see, therefore, that Gneivas Daas is violated even if there is a non-financial deception – in other words even if the honoree is not getting less money. The prohibition of deceiving is a clear out and out prohibition according to all opinions. According to the Sefer Yereim and the Ritvah it is a biblical prohibition. According to the SMaK the prohibition is derabanan. But all hold that it is a full blown prohibition.

There is a fascinating Shaarei Teshuva (3:181) which states that the leniency of "Mutar l'shanos mipnei haShalom, sometimes it is permitted to tell a white lie to maintain peace" does not apply to Gneivas Daas. Gneivas Daas is an important and essential value in Torah Judaism.

AN ILLUMINATING GEMORAH

The Gemorah in Rosh HaShana 26b records the following incident:

[Someone came and said,]

"John Doe blanked me!" [The word that he had used was, "keva'a."]

Levi did not understand what that man was saying to him. He did not know the meaning of the word, "kava'a."

He went and asked the meaning in the Beis Midrash. They said to him: That man said to you: He robbed me, as it is written: "Will a man rob [hayikba] G-d?" (Malachi 3:8).

Rava of Barnish said to Rav Ashi: Had I been there in Levi's place, I would have tried to uncover the meaning of the word in a different way. I would have said to him: "How did he keva'a you?

With what did he keva'a you? And why did he keva'a you?" And from his answers I would have understood on my own what was being said.

We see from this Gemorah that Rava of Barnish was suggesting a type of deception of sorts that would not be considered a prohibition of Gneivas Daas.

The operative definition of non-financial "Gneivas Da'as" according to the TaZ (Yore Deah 120:11) is where the deceiver receives a benefit of favor. It is where the person being deceived would feel that they owe you something. In Hebrew this term is called, "yachzik lo tovah." Since the deception here may involve someone doing someone else a favor

– it may be considered Gneivas Daas. The same would be true both in this Gemorah in Rosh HaShana.

IS IT LYING?

In regard to the verse (Shmos 23:7) in Parshas Mishpatim of "midvar sheker tirchak – stay away from a false matter," there is a three way debate as to how we understand this pasuk. The Chofetz Chaim rules in his Ahavas Chessed that there is an out and out prohibition to lie. This is in accordance with the view of some Rishonim. Other Rishonim hold that the verse is merely good advice, but not halacha. A third opinion holds that it is applicable to judges adjudicating law. Generally speaking, the view of the Chofetz Chaim is normative halacha.

But here, there is no actual lie being said – it is just that the person placing the ad is misleading the other. The Targum Unkelus, according to the Sefer Be'er Moshe, translates the verse as meaning – regarding falsehoods look at it as something disgusting to stay far away from.

It could be, however, that everyone knows that it is being done – so it may not be a violation of midvar sheker tirchak.

EVEN FURTHER

Perhaps the person placing the ad cannot afford it, and doing this is a form of lying mipnei hashalom.

The Gemorah in Yevamos 65b is the source for the idea of lying for the sake of Shalom. The Gemorah cites Rabbi Eelaah in the name of Rabbi Elazar the son of Rabbi Shimon. Rabbi Elazar derives this principle – that one may "change" to maintain the peace from the fact that the brothers told Yoseph that Yaakov their father had instructed them to tell Yoseph to forgive their sin against him. In fact, Yaakov did not leave any such instruction.

Rav Nosson even goes further – it is not just that permission is granted – it is even a Mitzvah! How do we know this? Because Hashem instructed Shmuel the prophet to lie to Shaul the king by telling him that he was bringing something to slaughter to Hashem. In fact, Shmuel was going to anoint Dovid as king in his stead.

It seems that Rabbi Elazar and Rabbi Nosson are not in agreement with each other but are actually arguing. Rabbi Elazar says that one may lie for the sake of peace. Rabbi Nosson says that it is a Mitzvah to do so.

The Eliyahu Rabbah OC 156 understands this Gemorah in this way too – that they are taking opposite positions.

Do we pasken, rule, like Rabbi Nosson? The Chofetz Chaim (Hilchos Rechilus 1:14) rules that we do rule that it is a Mitzvah. He is not alone. The Rif in Yevamos and in Bava Metziah 13a quotes our Gemorah and clearly rules in accordance with Rabbi Nosson. The Rosh in Yevamos 6:21 also rules like Rabbi Nosson and the Ohr Zaruah BM 3:63 does so as well.

So we see that not only may it be permitted in such case, when there is a Mitzvah to perform, Rav Nosson holds that it is a Mitzvah and it looks like we rule in accordance with Rav Nosson.

CONCLUSIONS

The conclusions may be vastly different. These ads depend upon the situation. If the person chiseling can afford it – it may be a genaivas daas. If he cannot – it may be a Mitzvah.

One last thought: There is another understanding of the verse. MiDvar Sheker – Regarding something that is a lie – tirchak – you will become distant – that is you will end up being distant from Hashem – Whose signet ring is truth. The goal of our life here on earth is to do Hashem's Will and emulate Him to the greatest extent that we can.

45054749R00139

Made in the USA
Middletown, DE
16 May 2019